KINDER KOLLEGE

Language Arts Spelling

Pre-K and Kindergarten

L. M. Logan
Patrice Juah
Ophelia S. Lewis

Village Tales Publishing
MINNEAPOLIS, MN

Copyright © 2020 by Liberia Literary Society.

All rights reserved. No part of this publication may be reproduced, distributed or transmitted in any form or by any means, without prior written permission.

Village Tales Publishing
www.villagetalespublishing.com
www.oass.villagetalespublishing.com
www.villagetalespublishing.com/childrensbooks

Book Cover & format by OASS

ISBN: 9781945408274
LCCN: 2020905086

A Liberia Literary Society Educational Project

Printed in the USA

This book belongs to:

____

How to care for your book.

1. Read with clean hands.
2. Turn pages carefully.
3. Keep your book in your bookbag when you're not reading it.
4. Keep your book close to you when reading, so that you don't drop it.
5. Use a bookmark to save your page in a book.
6. Keep your book away from food and drinks.
7. Only draw, write, and color where instructed to.
8. Keep your book away from younger siblings and pets.

Primary Handwriting Guidelines

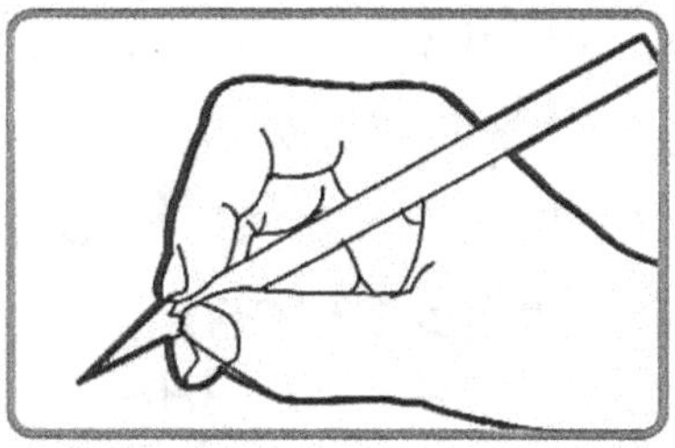

Sit down and place book flat in front of you.	Use your helper hand to hold the paper down while writing.	Correctly hold your pencil; only move the fingers when writing.

Contents

Writing and Spelling.......7
UPPERCASE.......8
lowercase.......9
Spell My First Name.......10
Spell My Last Name.......11
I Can Learn My 2-Letter Words.......12
Pyramids.......14
I Can Build 2-Letter Words Pyramids 15
I Can Learn My 3-Letter Words.......26
Alphabetical Order.......33
Rhyming.......37
Maze Rhymes.......41
Rhyme and Reason.......42
Perfect Pairs.......43
Rhyming Time.......44
Odd Rhyme Out.......45
Perfect Pairs Too.......46
Word Search.......47
4-Letter Words.......55
Rhyming Butterflies.......59
Build-a-Word.......60
Odd One Out.......62
5-Letter Words.......80
6-Letter Words.......91
Trace your 7-Letter Words.......97
7-Letter Pyramids.......98
Trace your 8-Letter Words.......100

Let's Write Some Christmas Words 103
Number Words 104
Color Words 106
My Color Words 110
Patriotic Words 111
Rainy Season 112
Social Relations 113
Fruits & Vegetables 115
Here Are Some Nuts 119
Things At The Beach 120
Weather Words 121
Body Parts 122
Opposite 123
Clothing Words 125
Let's Eat 126
Months Of The Year 129
7 Days A Week 131
School Days 134
Write Your School Supply List 135
Graduation Words 138
Word Smart Puzzles 149
Animals At The Zoo 150
Animals In The Water 151
Animals On The Farm 152
Bugs & Insects 153
Pets 154
Food 155
Fruits and Veggies 156
Transportation 157
School Things 158

Going Shopping 159
How Do You Feel Today? 160
I Love My Family 163
Family Words 164

Writing and Spelling

Begin With The Alphabet

UPPERCASE

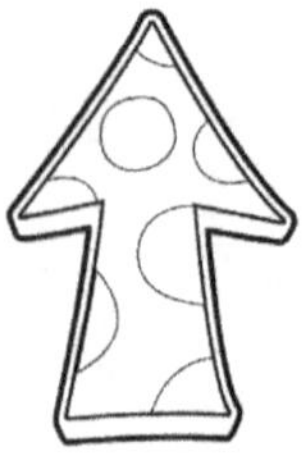

A B C D E

F G H I J K

L M N O P

Q R S T U

V W X Y Z

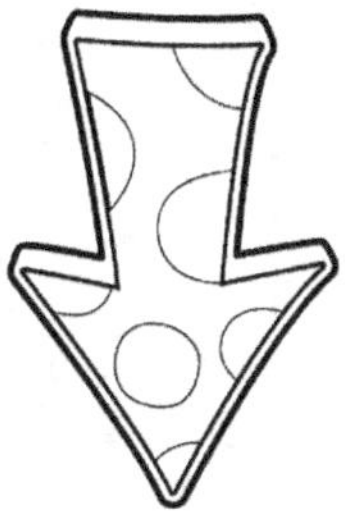

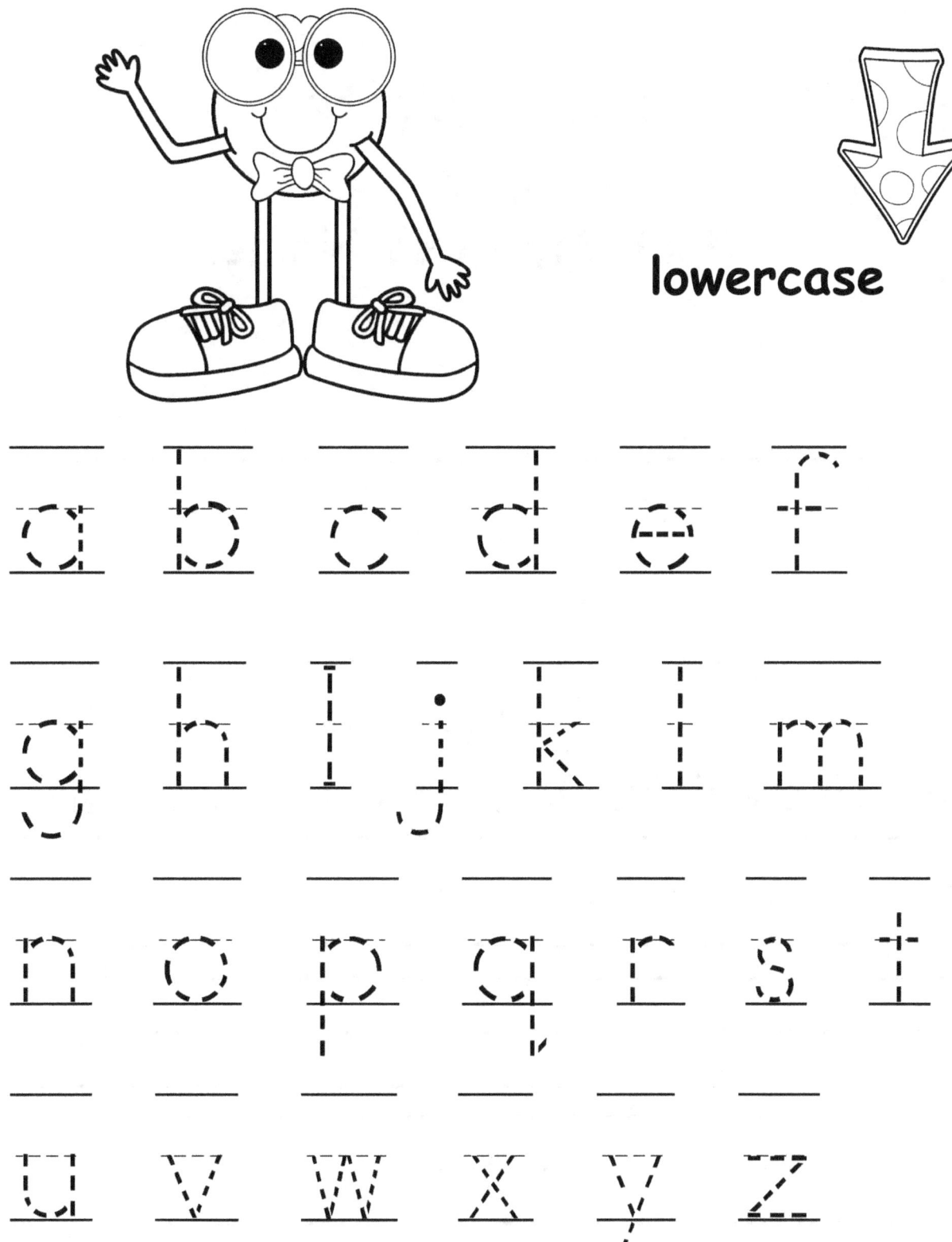

lowercase

a b c d e f

g h i j k l m

n o p q r s t

u v w x y z

I Can Write
and
Spell My First Name

☐ ☐ ☐ ☐ ☐ ☐ ☐ ☐ ☐ ☐

Pratice writing your first name 3 times.

I Can Write
and
Spell My Last Name

□ □ □ □ □ □ □ □ □ □

Pratice writing your last name 3 times.

I Can Learn My 2-Letter Words

am
or
as
of
at
be
go
me
he

up
hi
if
an
my
is
ax
it
no

on
do
in
ox
so
to
by
us
we
Mr.
Dr.
Ms.
TV

Trace each word.

lower case

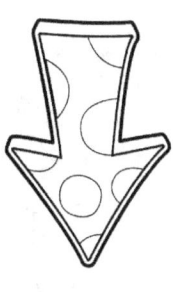

am	it
or	no
as	on
of	do
at	in
be	ox
go	so
me	to
he	bY
up	us
hi	we
if	
an	
mY	
is	
ax	

UPPERCASE

AM	
OR	IS
AS	AX
OF	IT
AT	NO
BE	ON
GO	DO
ME	IN
HE	OX
UP	SO
HI	TO
IF	BY
AN	US
MY	WE

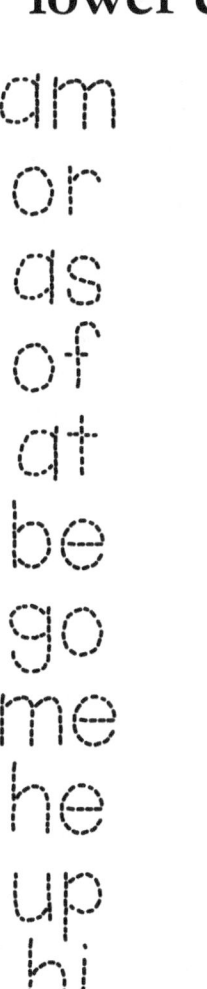

Building Pyramids With Words

Write your spelling word one letter at a time. Follow the example.

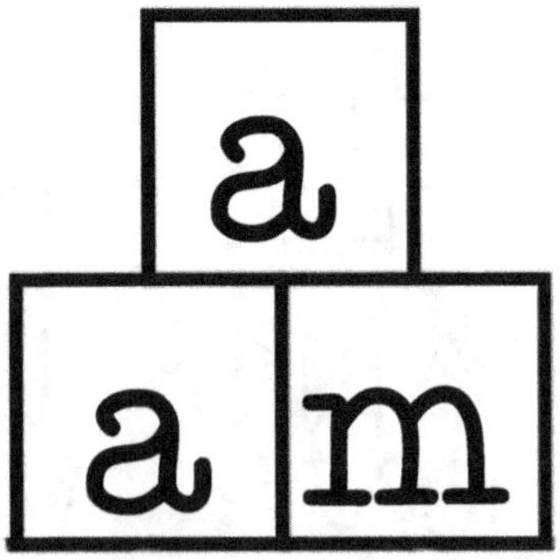

a m

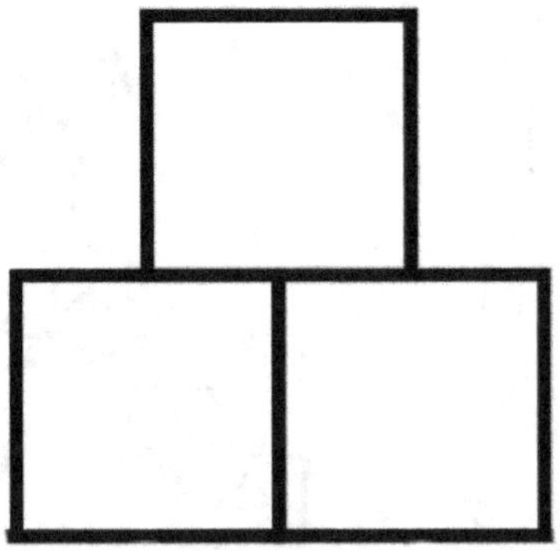

I Can Build 2-Letter Words Pyramids

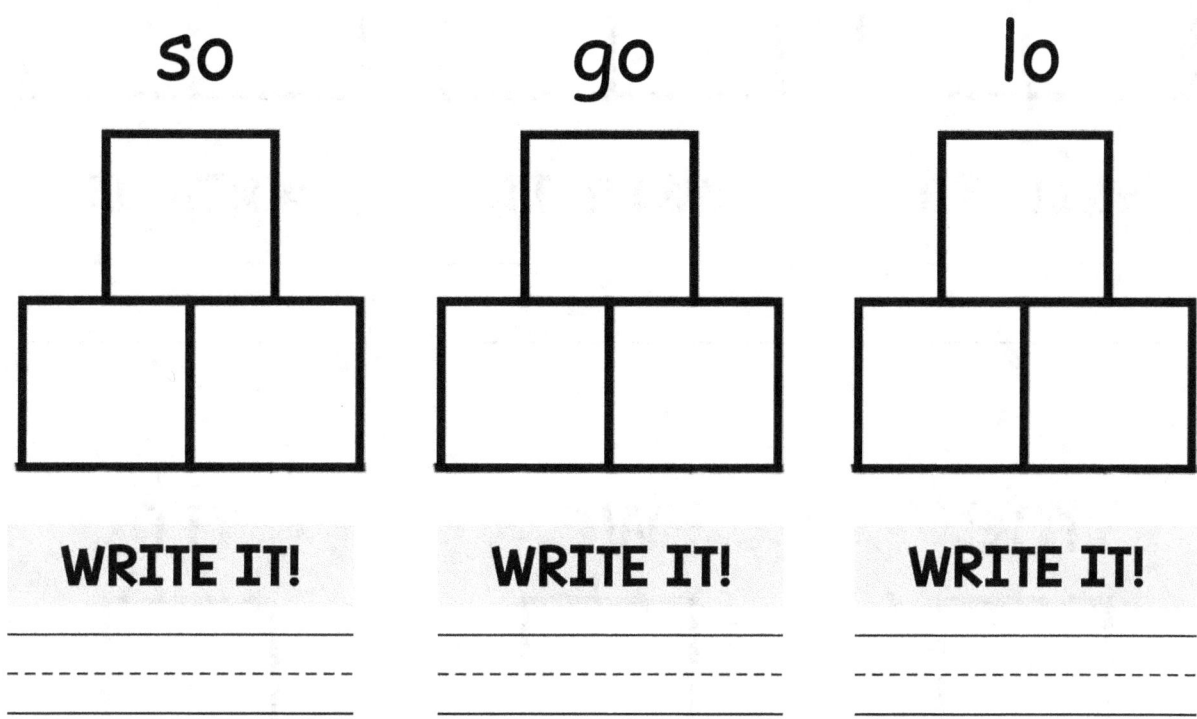

so

WRITE IT!

go

WRITE IT!

lo

WRITE IT!

no

WRITE IT!

he

WRITE IT!

be

WRITE IT!

me

WRITE IT!

we

WRITE IT!

at

WRITE IT!

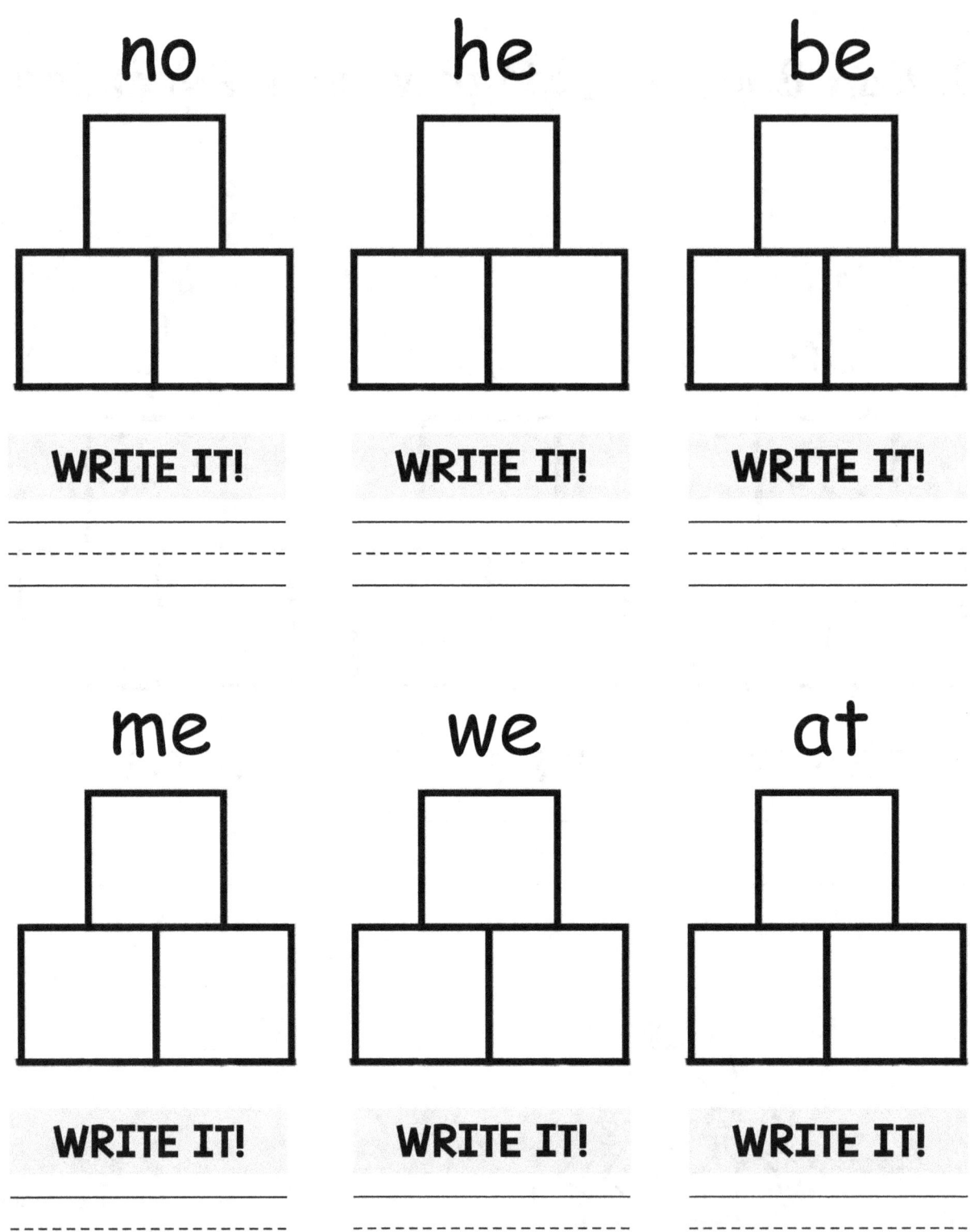

an

WRITE IT!

a m

WRITE IT!

a s

WRITE IT!

if

WRITE IT!

is

WRITE IT!

it

WRITE IT!

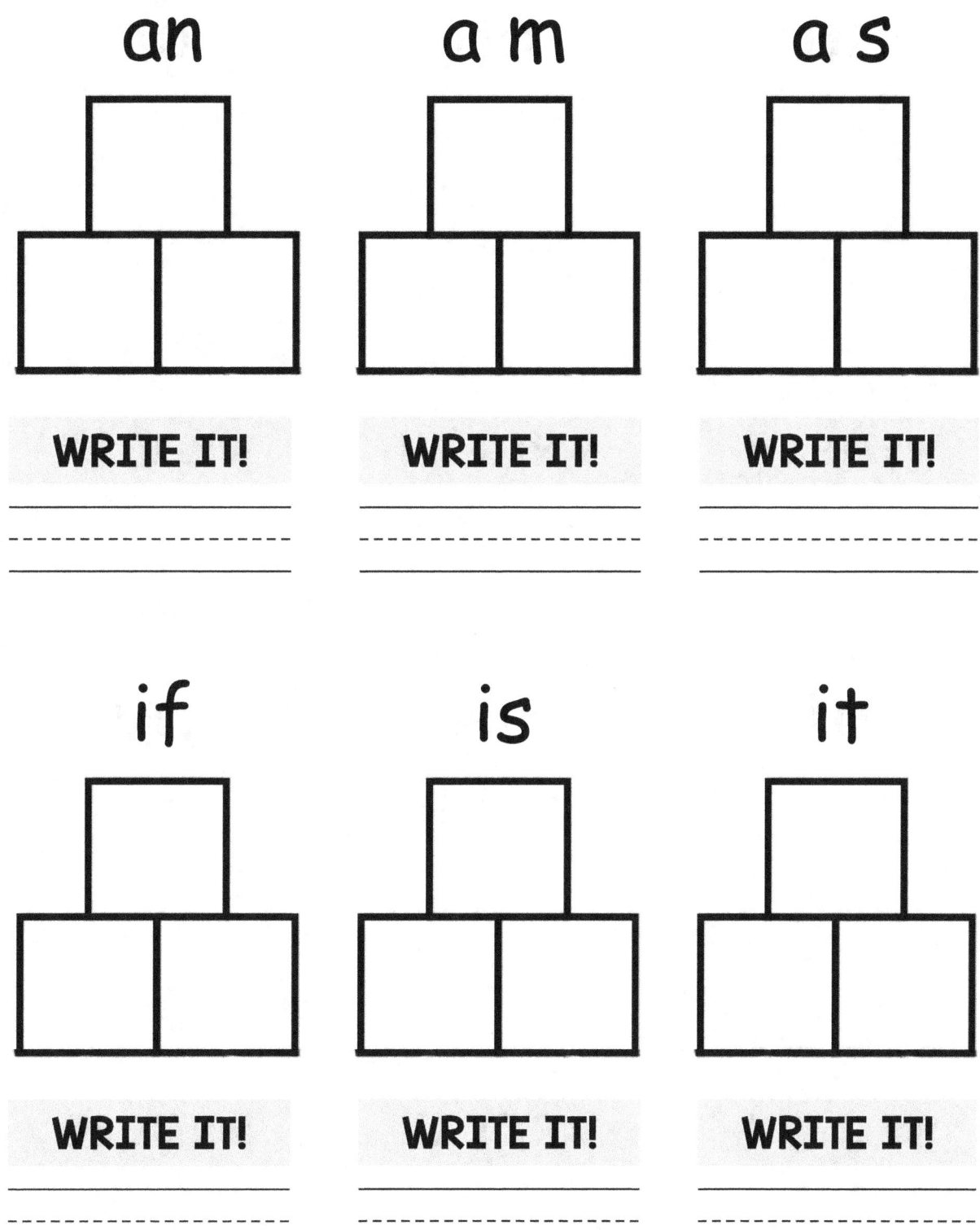

in

WRITE IT!

on

WRITE IT!

or

WRITE IT!

of

WRITE IT!

ox

WRITE IT!

by

WRITE IT!

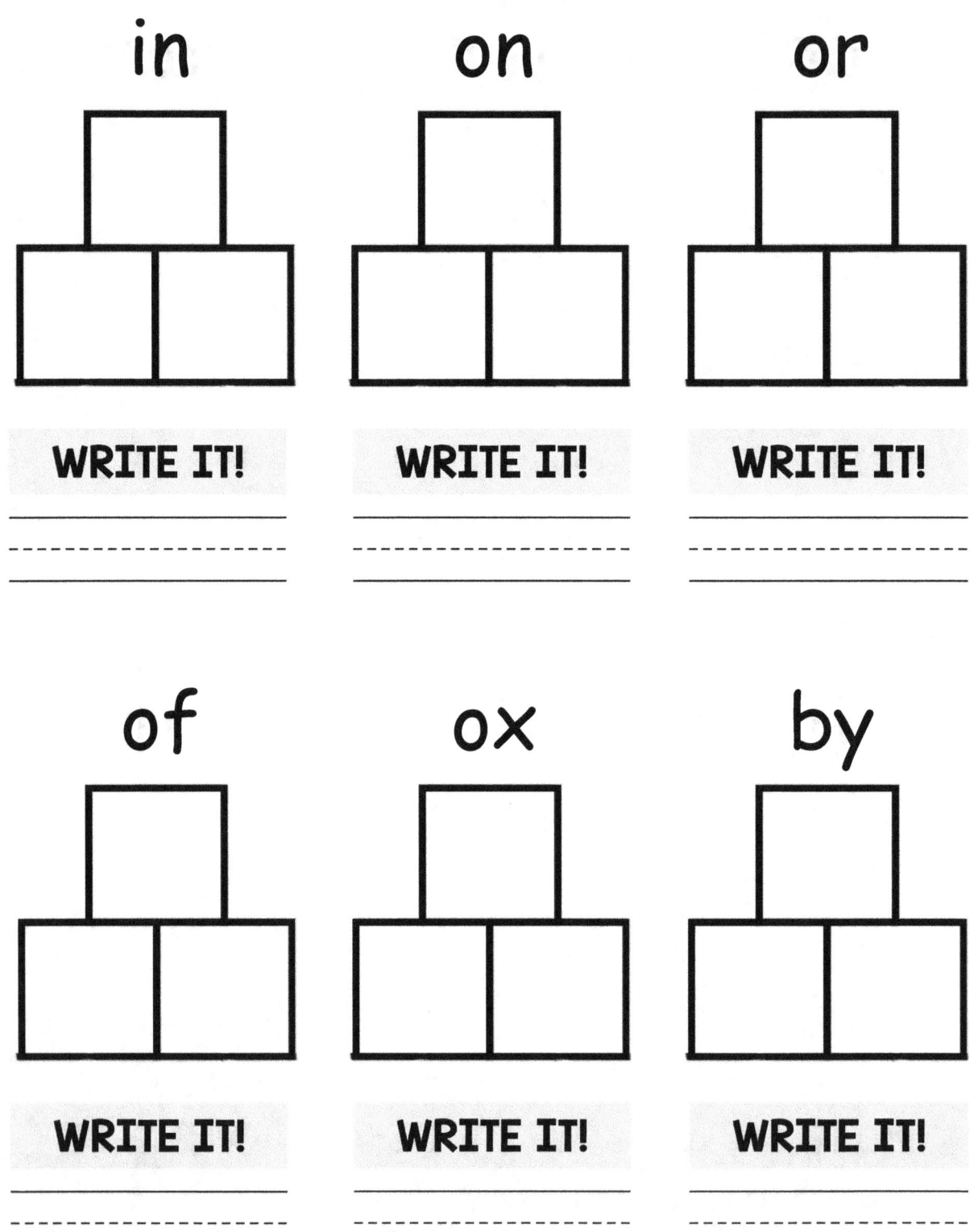

my

WRITE IT!

up

WRITE IT!

us

WRITE IT!

to

WRITE IT!

do

WRITE IT!

Good Job!

No Peeking!	I can write all my 2-letter words

Write your favorite
2-letter words here.

Name:______________________________

Name:____________________________

Name: ______________________________

Name:_______________________________

I Can Learn My 3-Letter Words

eat
act
air
any
ate
his
bad
ban
bat

bay
bed
bee
pat
top
get
two
use
pad

cap
him
car
gee
hot
pin
out
cry
wax

rob
job
Mrs.
fan
has
nap
six
sky
low
off
our
pal
pay
pop
pot

Let's build more pyramids with 3-letter words.

Write your spelling words one letter at a time. Follow the example.

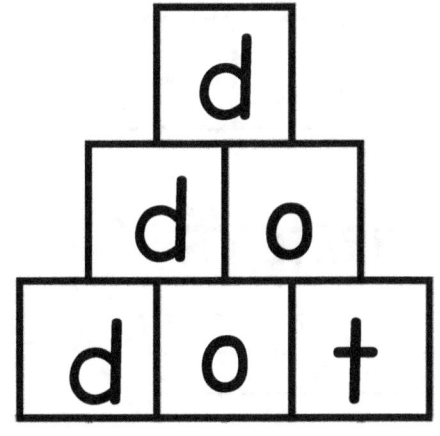

dot

d
d o
d o t

few

WRITE IT!

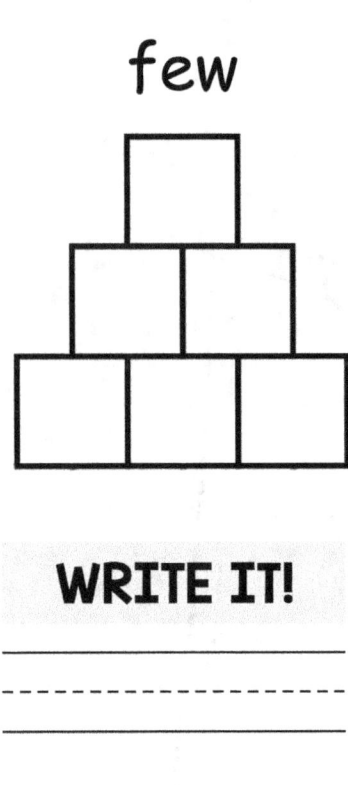

owl	may
few	lit
zip	toe
you	pan
old	new
egg	hay
not	yea

owl

WRITE IT!

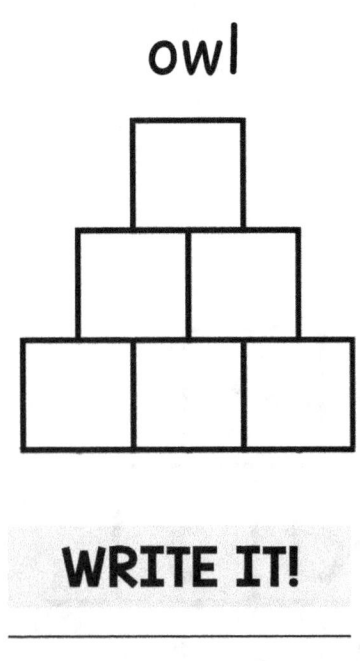

tap	cup
set	dam
ant	had
say	
wed	
one	
and	

zip

you

old

WRITE IT!

WRITE IT!

WRITE IT!

egg

not

may

WRITE IT!

WRITE IT!

WRITE IT!

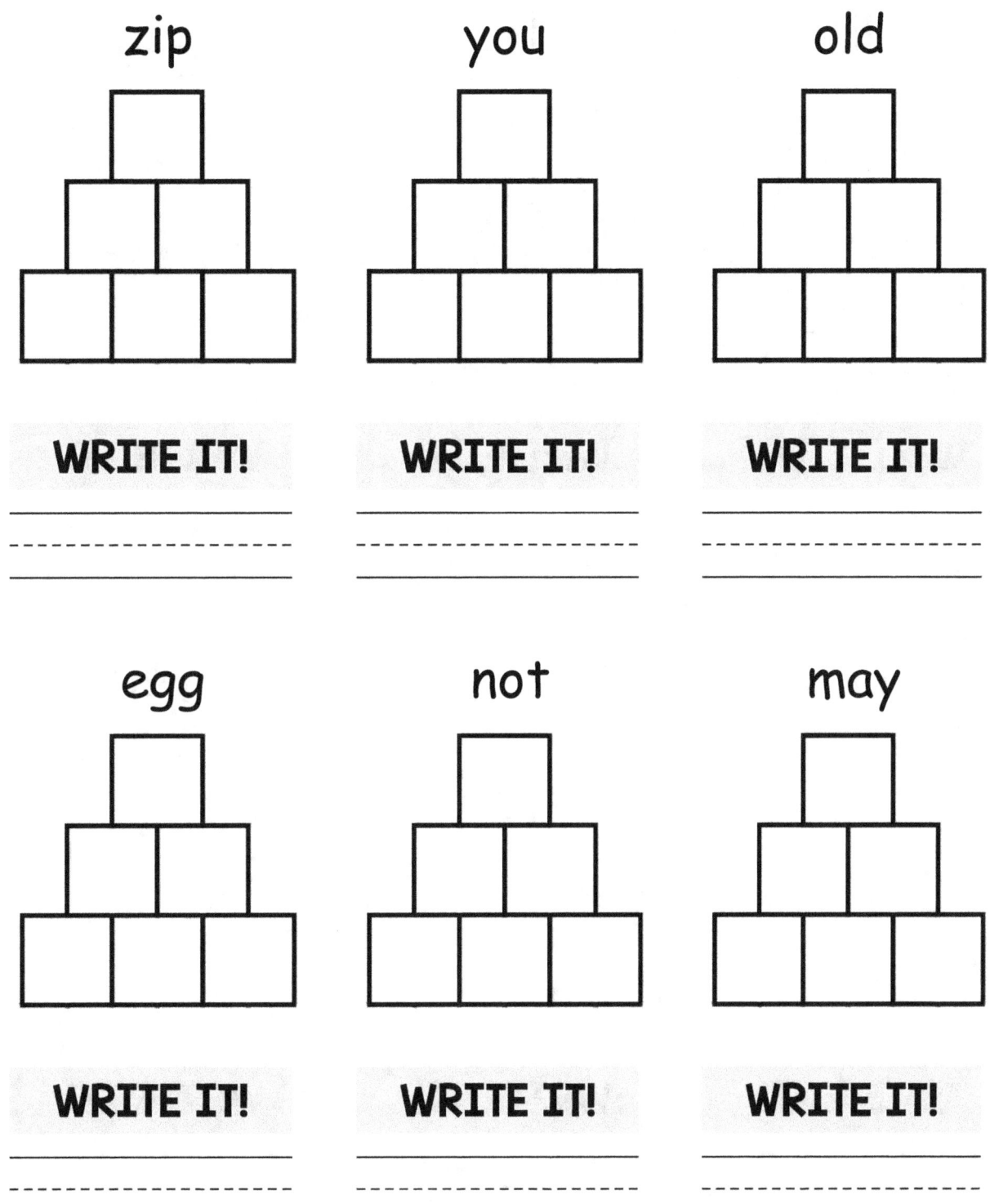

lit

toe

pan

WRITE IT!

WRITE IT!

WRITE IT!

new

hay

yea

WRITE IT!

WRITE IT!

WRITE IT!

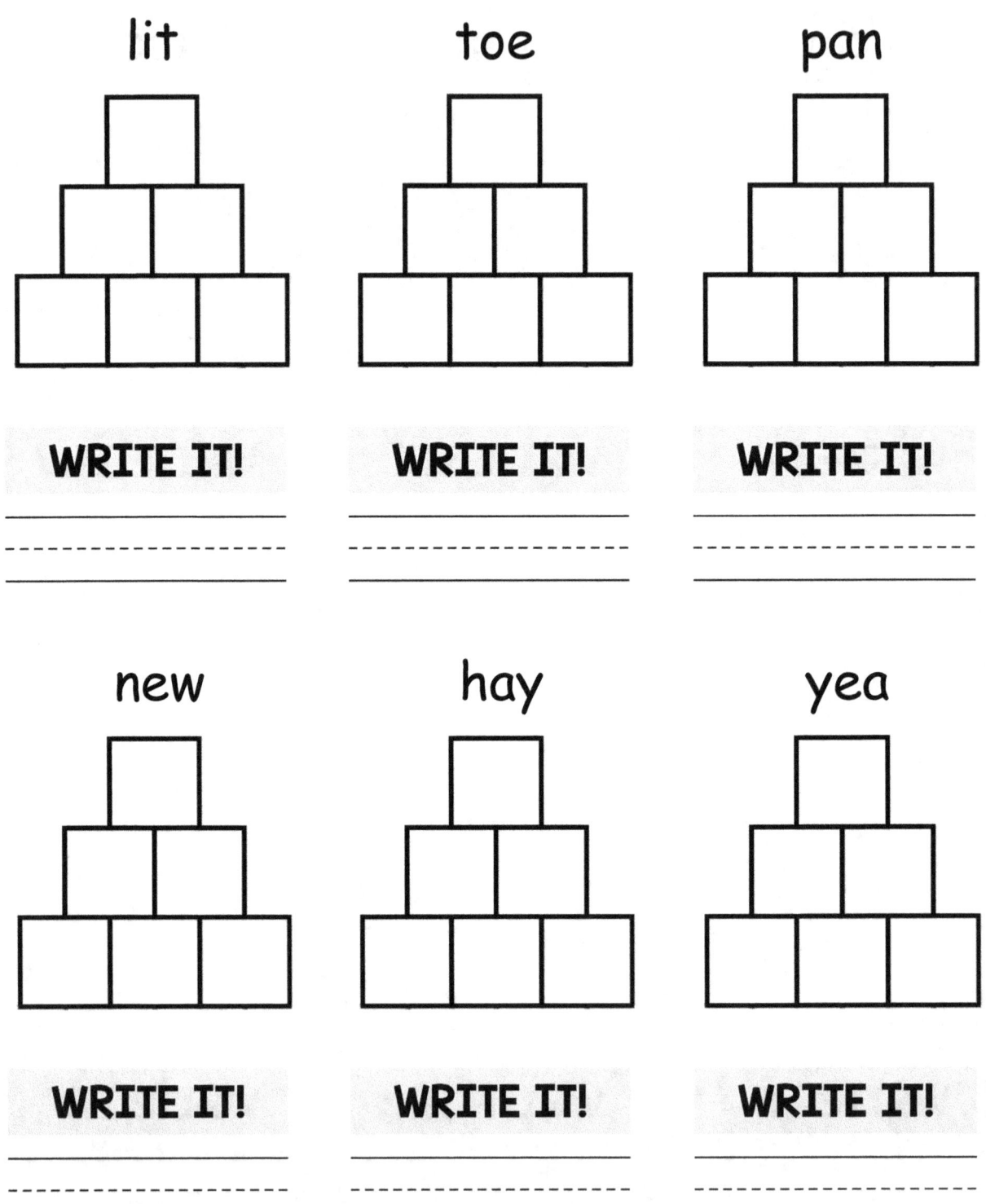

tap

WRITE IT!

set

WRITE IT!

ant

WRITE IT!

say

WRITE IT!

wed

WRITE IT!

one

WRITE IT!

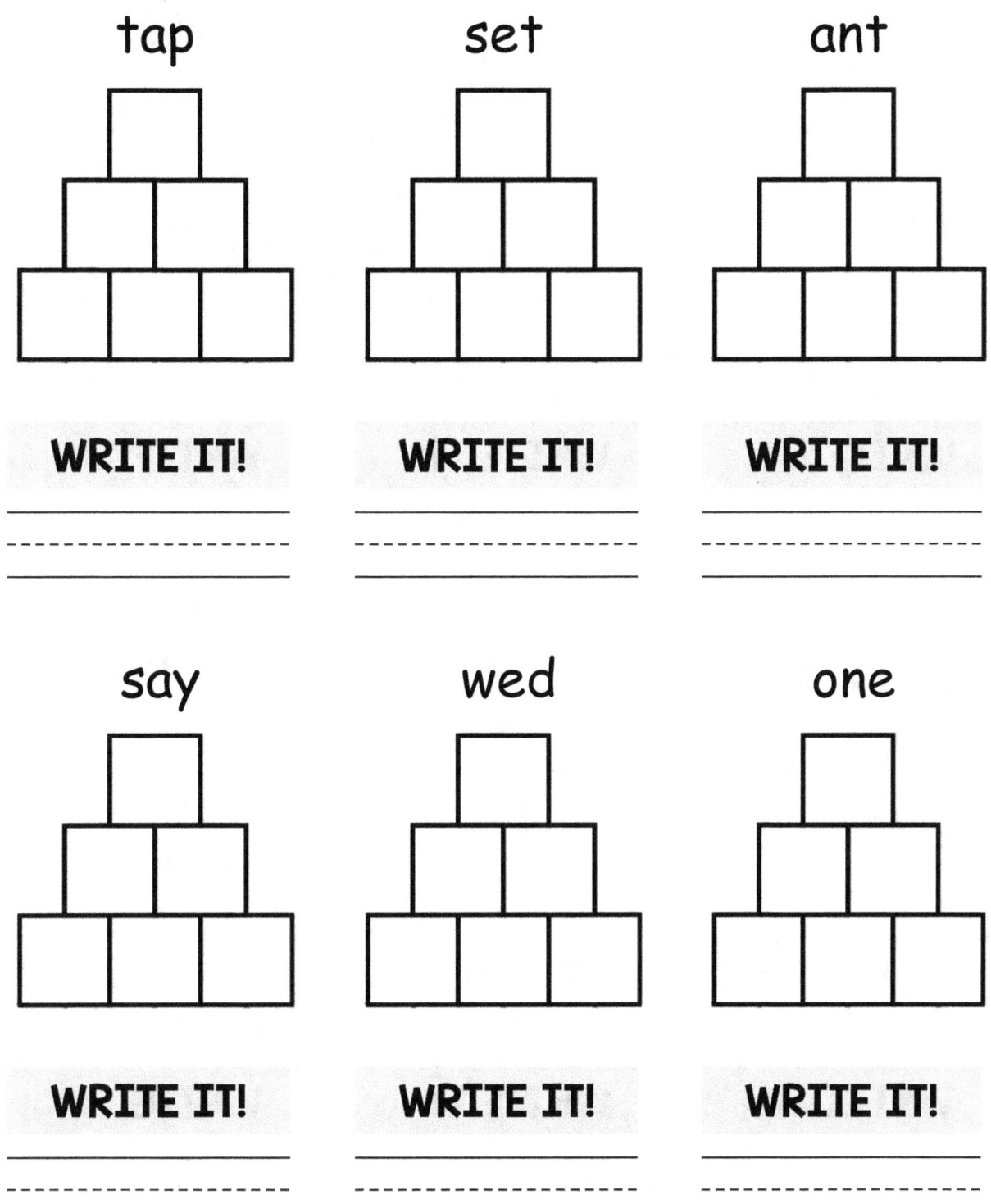

and

WRITE IT!

cup

WRITE IT!

dam

WRITE IT!

had

WRITE IT!

boo

WRITE IT!

did

WRITE IT!

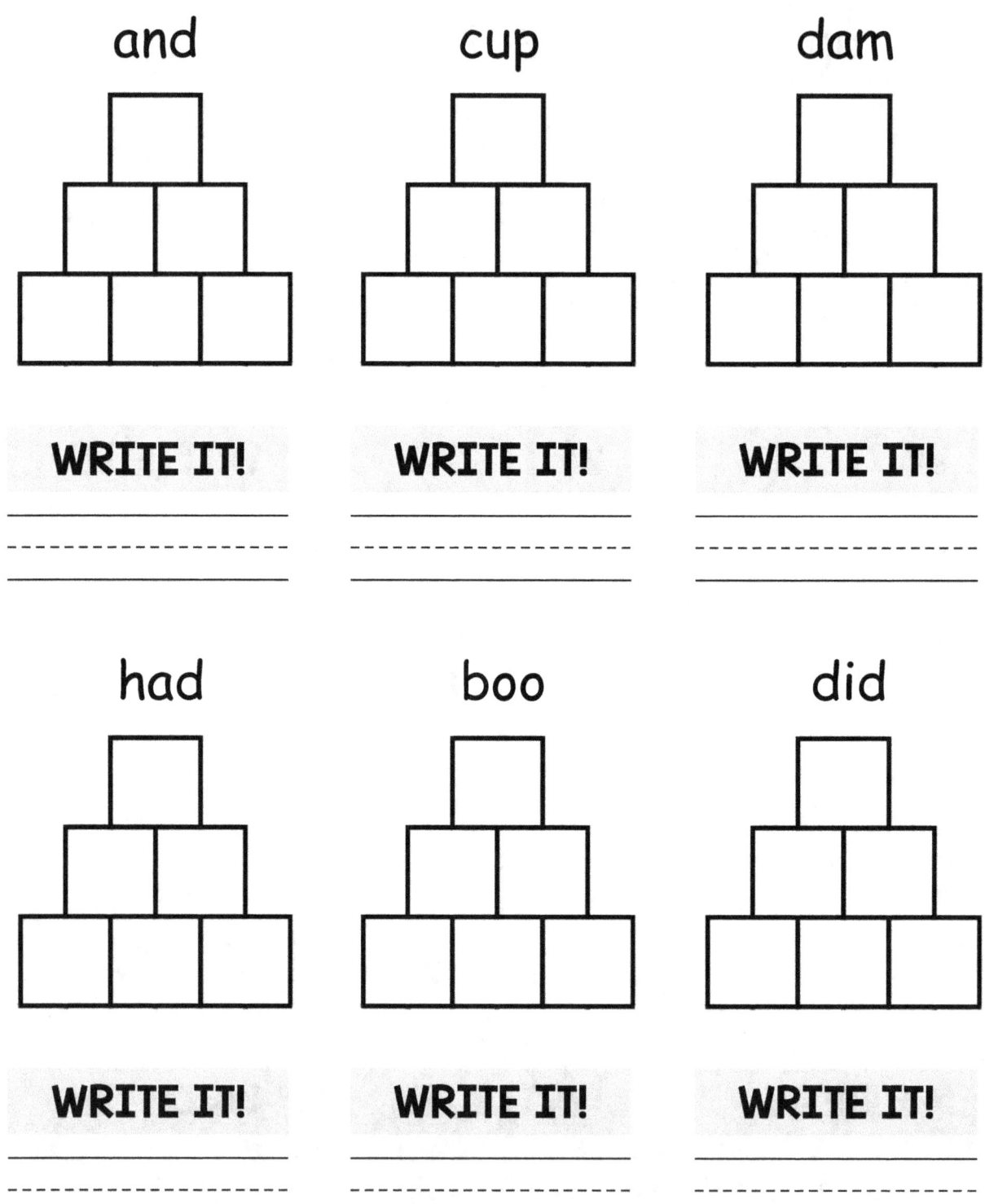

Alphabetical Order

I can write my words in alphabetical order

Write your spelling words in ABC order.

day
van
row
ten
hen
leg
now
red
bus

eye
win
zoo
jet
man
pie
sad
yes
ice
cow

oil
try
fun
gum
key
arm

Which letter is missing?

WRITE IT!

Color Koko Koloko
with your favorite colors.

Rhyming

Find the words that rhyme in your spelling list.

	cut	
toy	mad	big
yam	wet	nut
mat	but	boy
hog	bug	ram
cat	log	hug
why	pig	shy
	hut	ham
	buy	dog
	add	bet
	let	joy
	mug	sad
	hat	wig

Add rhyming words to match the picture.

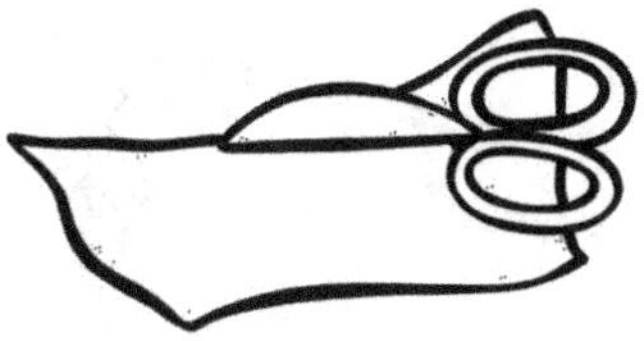

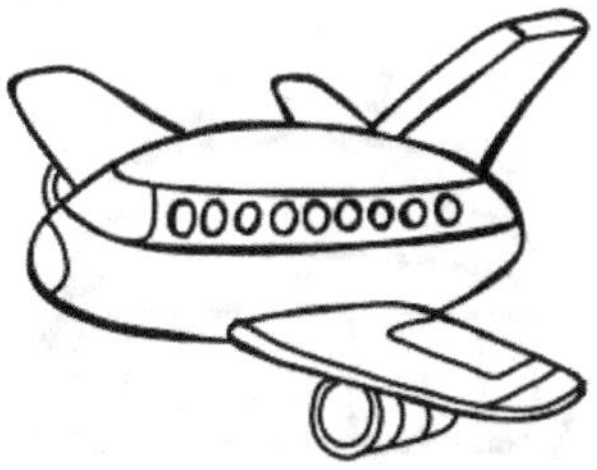

Add rhyming words to match the picture.

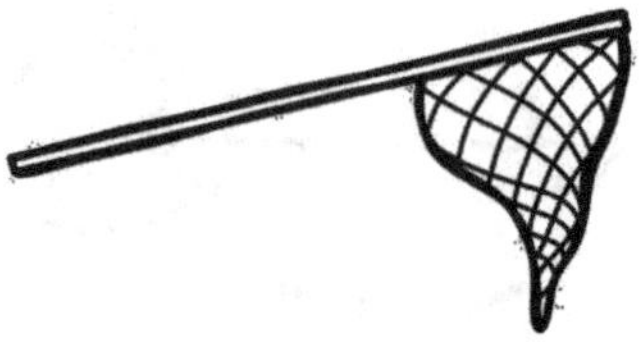

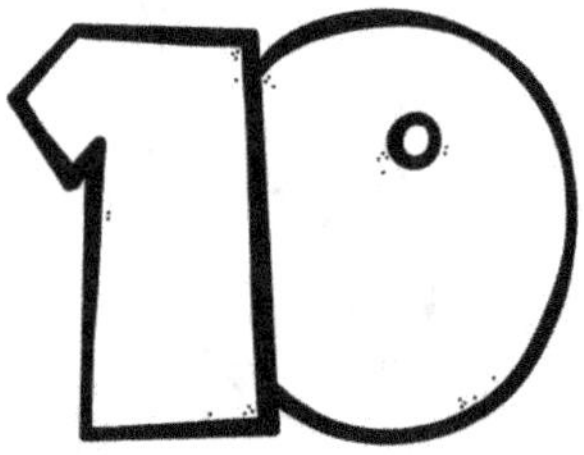

Maze Rhymes

Find and color the rhyming words to get from START to FINISH.

START	fat	jet	mug	bar	jam
car	cat	bat	win	bug	net
van	pen	mat	log	win	pot
pod	fin	hat	rat	pat	pop
cup	ran	fan	wig	sat	FINISH

Rhyme and Reason

1. big
2. ham
3. log
4. fox
5. toy
6. nut
7. mat
8. hug

Write the number next to the picture they rhyme with.

Perfect Pairs

Draw a line from each picture on the left to the picture that rhymes with it on the right.

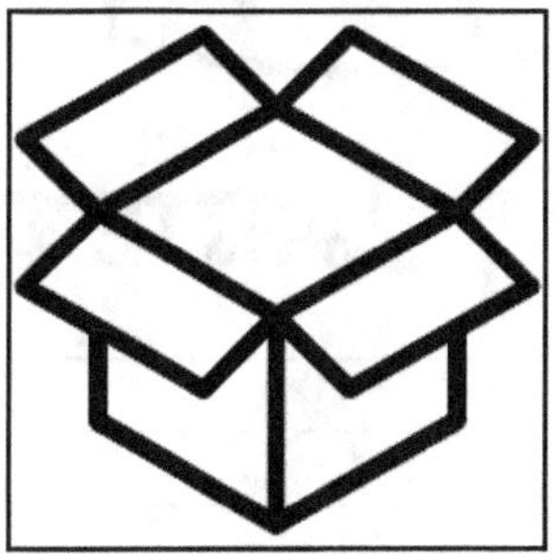

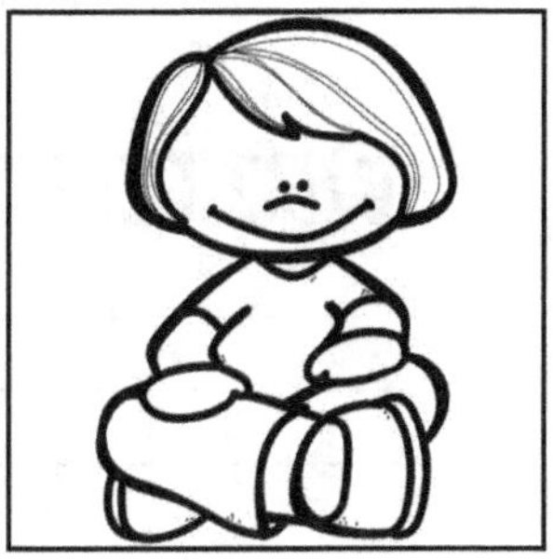

Rhyming Time

Write the word under each picture. Circle the rhyming word in the box next to each picture.

shy
bet
but

WRITE IT!

let
pan
add

WRITE IT!

why
hog
wet

WRITE IT!

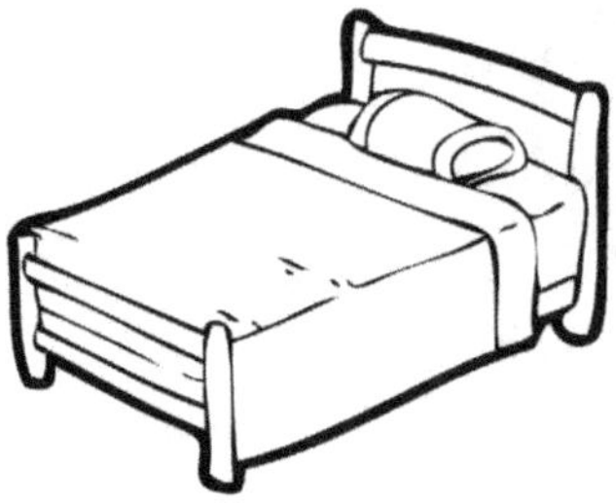

red
cut
mad

WRITE IT!

Odd Rhyme Out

Look at the first picture in each row, then circle the picture that does not rhyme with it.

Perfect Pairs Too

Draw a line from each word on the left, to the word that rhymes with it on the right.

pop	red
fin	bar
bed	hug
hot	hop
car	hum
hit	tin
bug	lot
gum	sit
bat	net
fig	log
met	sun
hog	cat
can	pan
bun	ten
dip	pig
men	hip

Word Search

Find the words in the spelling list, then circle each word in the puzzle.

put	saw	son	the
ran	sea	sun	was
rat	see	tag	way
rip	she	taz	who
run	sit		

s	e	a	h	s	i	t	m
w	y	p	u	t	e	m	s
w	a	s	s	t	r	e	a
w	r	y	u	h	a	a	w
h	z	u	n	e	t	b	n
o	b	s	n	w	s	a	n
r	i	p	o	l	h	m	z
t	a	g	v	n	e	w	w

3-letter
word List

eat	bat	use	out
act	bay	pad	cry
air	bed	cap	wax
any	bee	him	rob
ate	pat	car	job
his	top	gee	Mrs.
bad	get	hot	fan
ban	two	pin	has

Learn your spelling words.

nap
six
sky
low
off
our
pal
pay
pop
pot
boo
bug
buy
cab
can
cub
did
all

eel
end
fad
ape
are
art
ask
fed
fit
fly
for
fur
gap
got
gun
her
hey
hit

how
its
jar
kid
lad
lap
led
lot
put
ran
rat
rip
run
saw
sea
see
she
sit

son
sun
tag
taz
the
was
way
who
owl
few
zip
you
old
egg
not
may
dot
lit
toe
pan
new

hay	bus	hog	hug
yea	eye	cat	shy
tap	win	why	ham
set	zoo	cut	dog
ant	jet	mad	bet
say	man	wet	
wed	pie	but	
one	sad	log	
and	yes	pig	
cup	ice	hut	
dam	cow	fox	
had	oil	add	
day	try	let	
van	fun	mug	
row	gum	hat	
ten	key	big	
hen	arm	nut	
leg	toy	boy	
now	jam	box	
red	mat	ram	

Name:______________________________

Name:____________________________

Name:______________________________

Name:________________________________

4-Letter Words

also
away
baby
back
barn
bead
bear
been
beep
bend
bent
best
come
cost
crab

dark
drop
lion
lose
loss
more
move
neat
next
nine
only
open
over
play
read
rent

ride
rule
safe
said
seal
send
shoe
sick
side
soft
some
song
soon
star
stop
sure
tend
than
that
them

then
they
this
week
went
were
will
wish
word
work
worm
yard
your
duck
easy
ever
face
farm
feel
fill

find
fire
fish
foot
four
free
frog
from
game
gave
gift
gold
grow
hair
hand
hard
have
head
hear
hers

high
hill
hole
hope
hurt
jump
keep
kind
kite
king
ring
five
live
miss
kiss
call
tall
mall
wall
ball

fall
talk
walk
good
food
book
look
tell
sell
well
bell
cake
take
bake
down
town

bull
pull
full
name
same
help
calf
here
love
made
many
both
came
used
very
wait

told
girl
give
glad
goat
tree
true
want
wave
lost
meow
pole
poor
with
boat
wolf
meet
lamb
land
city

rice
road
room
cold
colt
last
late
lend
yell
zero
what
when
light
like
line

deer
doll
bird
blue
xray
boss
care
palm
sent
pass
door
dove
draw
rock

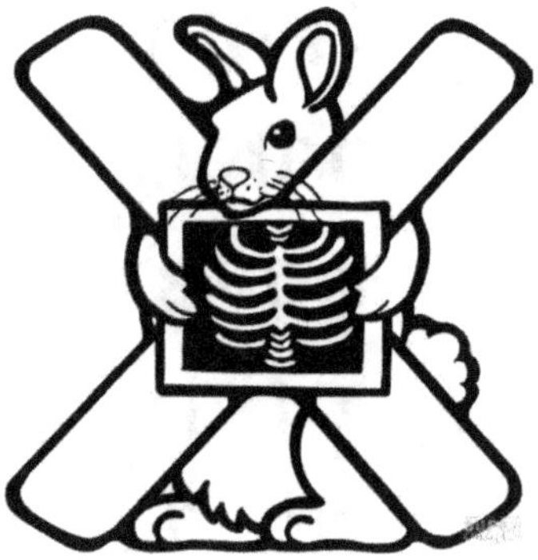

Rhyming Butterflies

Help Market Dog match the rhyming butterflies. Color the two rhyming butterflies using the same color.

miss

five talk ring call

tall good  kiss

food town look live

book king walk down

Build-a-Word

Make words by joining up the letters.

m b a r

a p b y

c b a r

v a k e

m a m r

l p b y

k b t r

a i b e

m b o c

a r q k

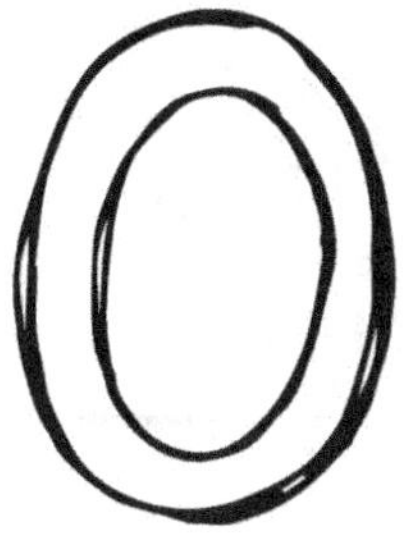

m e r o

z p b y

m c a r

d u k y

m u o o

a o b k

d a n r

h p k d

Odd One Out

Cross out the one that doesn't rhyme.

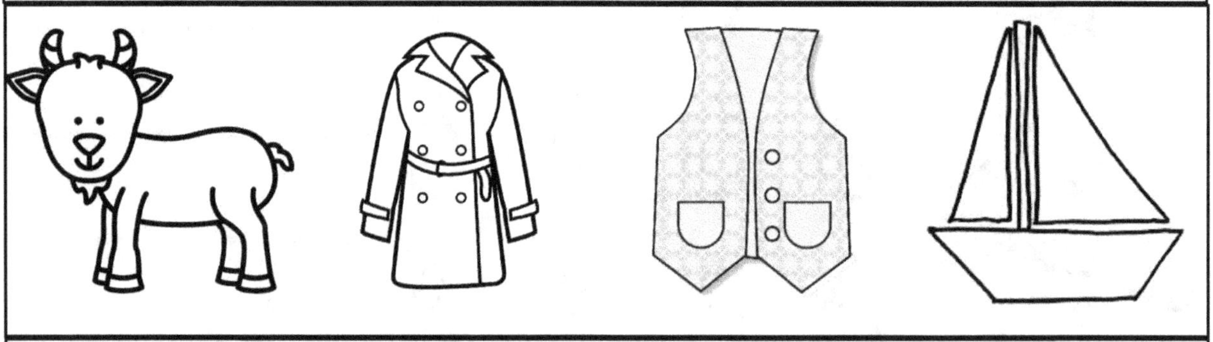

Write the names of the pictures you crossed out.

ram

frog

vest

Trace your spelling words.

jam lamp jeep

duck log sheep

goat coat clam

worm sleep frog

Read. Trace. Write.

Read each word. Trace and add the missing letter to each word. Write the word.

best	both	bell
_est	b_th	be_l

come	cold	city
co_e	_old	c_ty

door	drop	down
do_r	d_op	do_n
easy	ever	east
e_sy	_ver	e_st
foot	farm	food
f_ot	f_rm	_ood

Building 4-letter Pyramid words Is fun!

Write your spelling word one letter at a time. Follow the example.

find

f

f i

f i n

f i n d

Write the word.

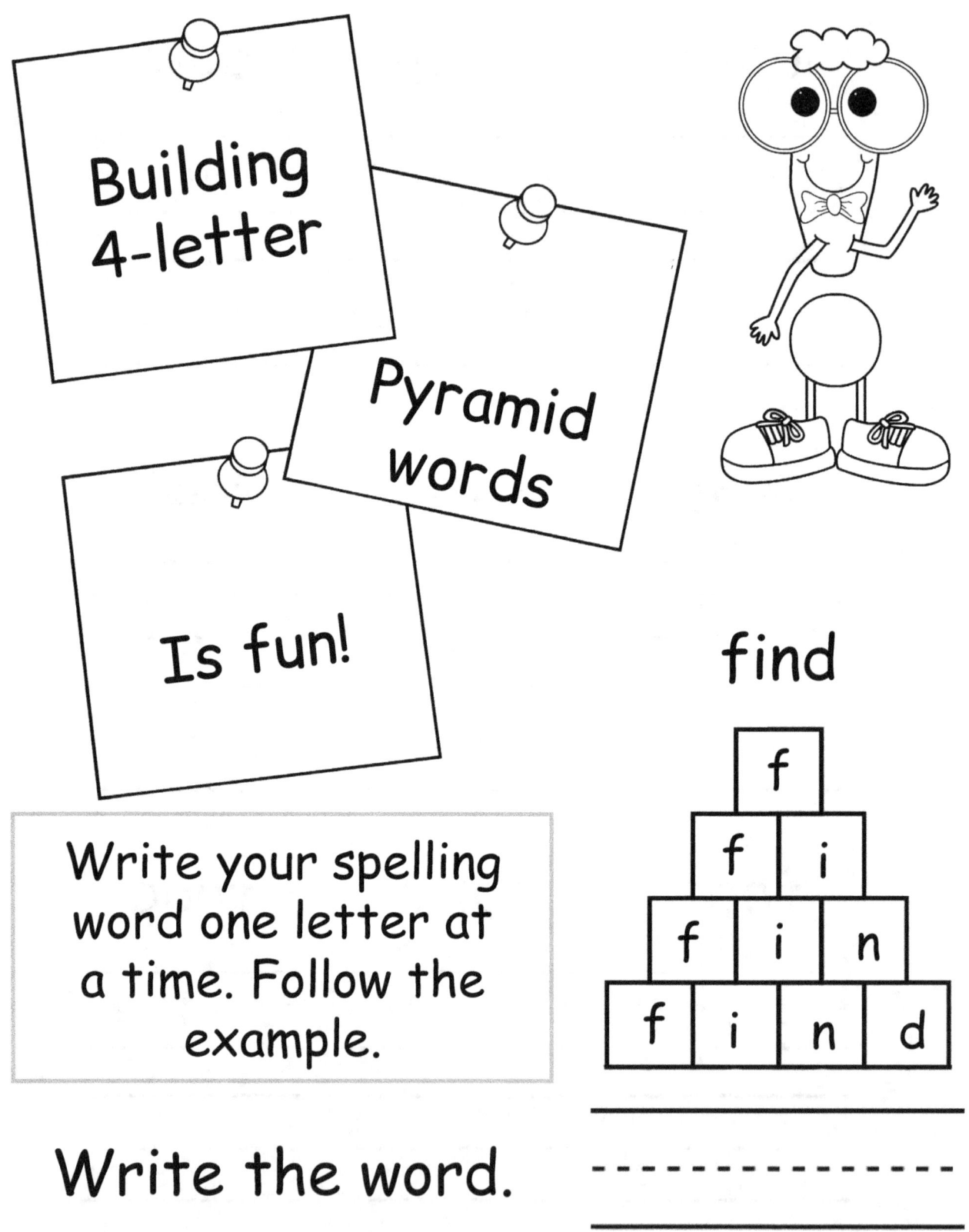

talk

tall

them

this

tree

wait

what

when

Use the word bank words to write them in the correct boxes.

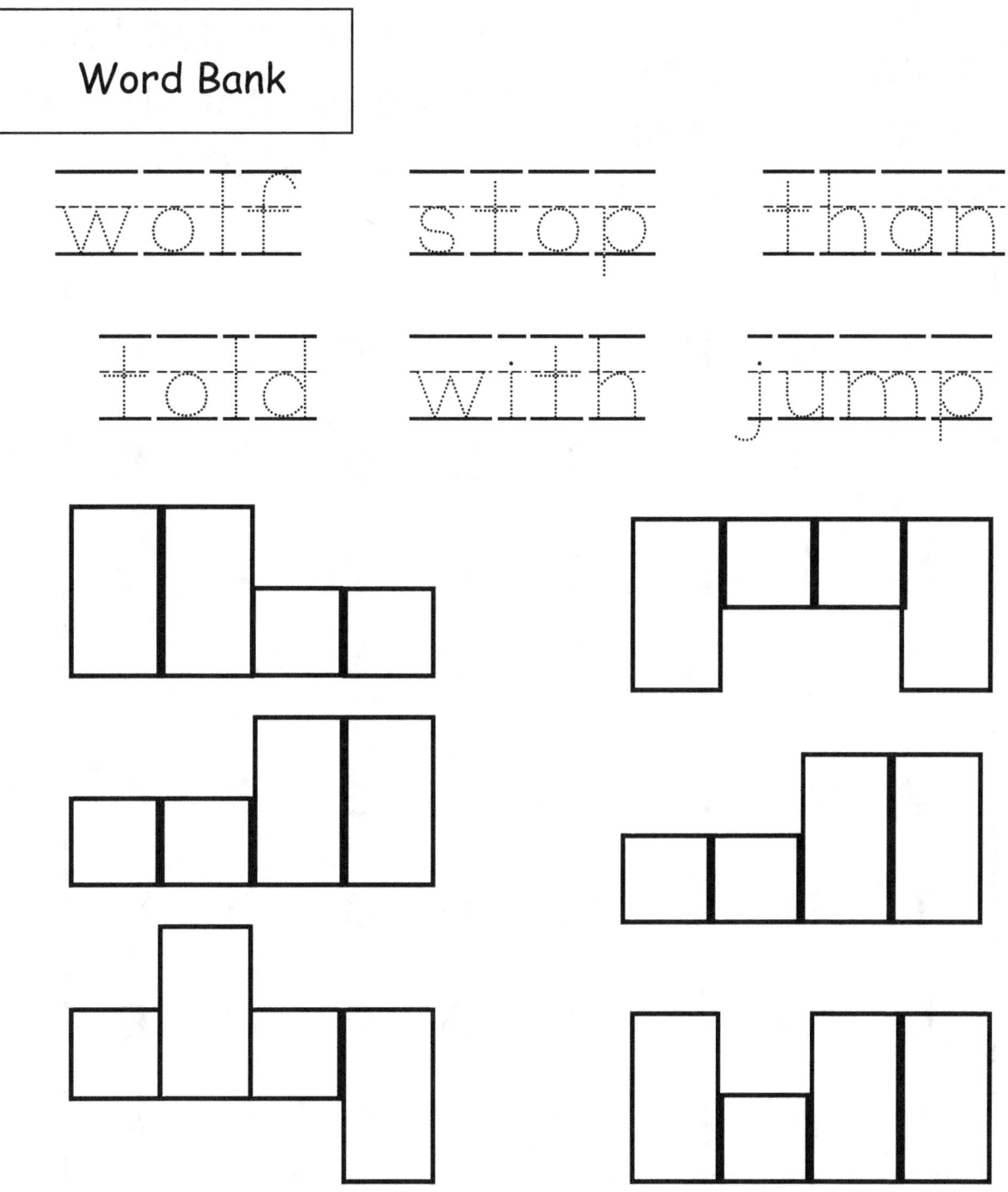

Word Bank

wolf stop than

told with jump

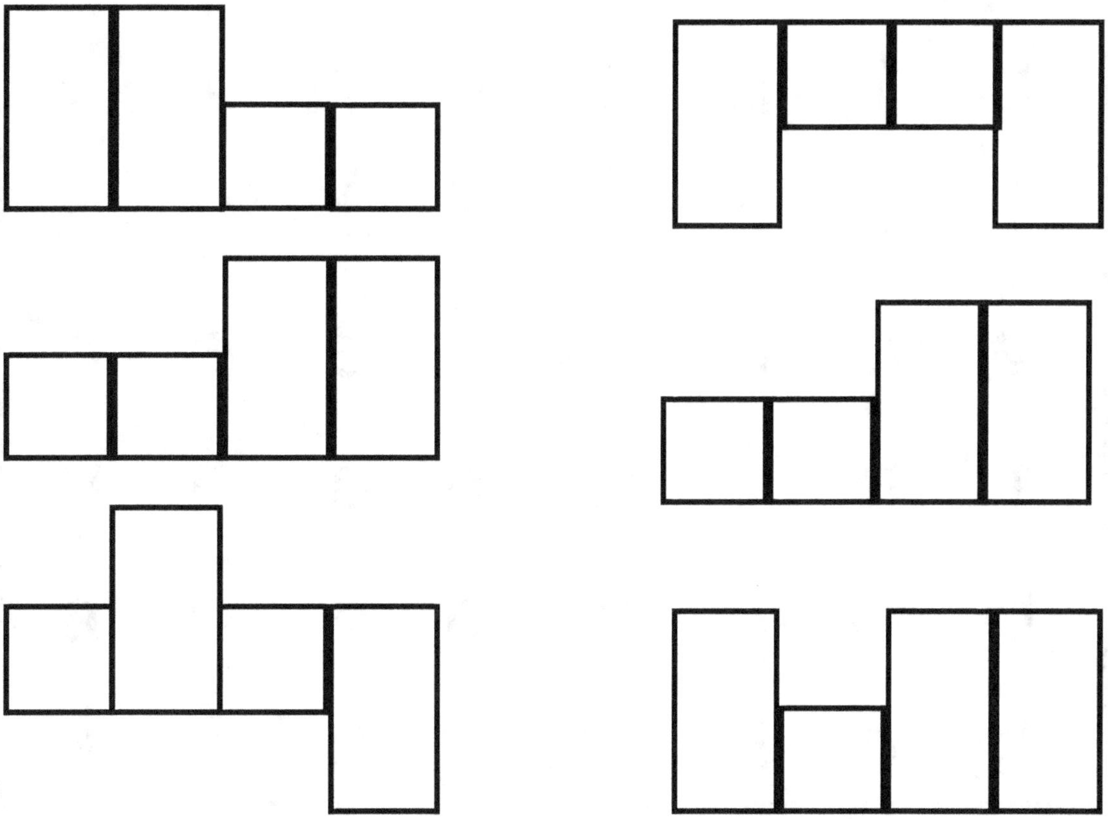

Word Bank

help	many
calf	both
here	came
love	used
made	very

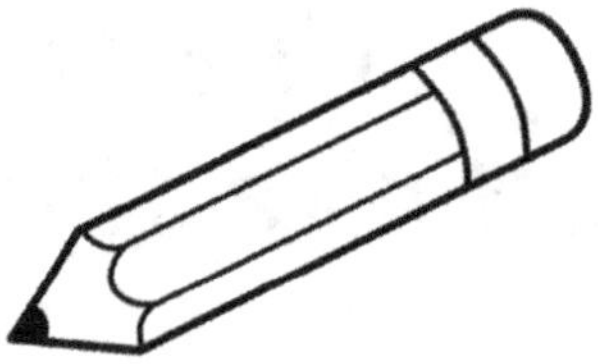

Circle each spelling word one time in the word search.

r	p	h	e	r	e	v	p
b	o	t	h	c	a	m	e
b	t	c	a	l	f	x	v
j	l	o	v	e	t	v	z
v	e	r	y	u	s	e	d
t	n	l	k	m	a	n	y
b	m	n	z	m	a	d	e
n	r	h	e	l	p	l	k

Write the word 4 times

Circle the word **beep** each time you see it.

beep week sure been

fire tell beep come

soon beep feel have

beep game beep

true love next poor

Put these 4-letter words in ABC order.

lamb
land
city
river
road
room
cold
colt
last
late
lend
yell
zero
what
when
light
fish
line
deer
doll
bird

blue
boss
care
palm
sent
pass
door
star
draw
rock

Color the pictures

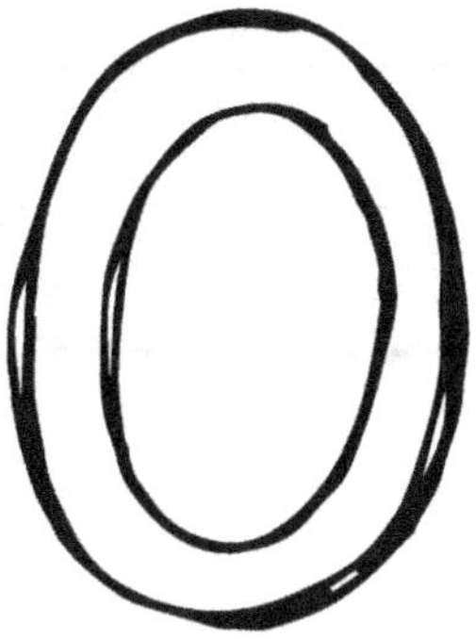

Write the word 4 times

Circle the word **crab** each time you see it.

only draw face late

crab meet crab sell

last head pass sick

crab move crab ride

soft same room

Write the word 4 times

Circle the word **stop** each time you see it.

give stop girl mall

song here town came

stop boat call kind

work help yard

stop kiss stop STOP

Name:______________________________

Name:____________________________

Name:________________________

Name:

5-Letter
Words

More spelling words to learn.

about	white	clean	hello
above	witch	color	house
after	woman	count	large
small	write	daddy	moose
stick	zebra	dream	music
store	alone	dress	nurse
story	apple	eight	paper
swim	beach	every	party
table	begin	fight	plate
these	black	floor	price
thing	bring	ghost	round
three	brown	goose	seven
tiger	camel	grass	sheep
train	candy	green	skunk
tried	carry	heart	

Let's
build some
5-letter
Pyramid words

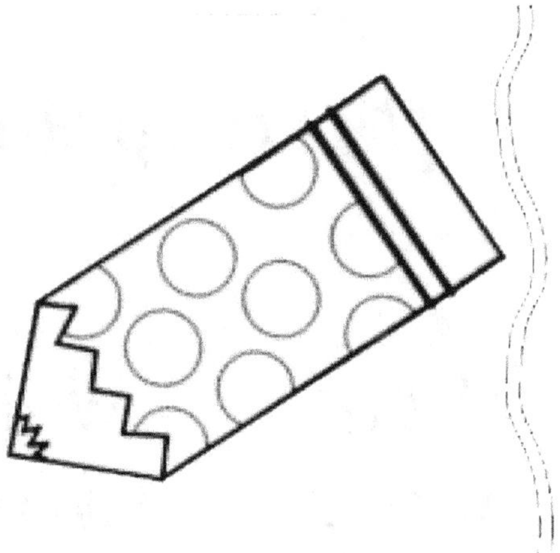

Write your spelling word one letter at a time. Follow the example.

river

r				
r	i			
r	i	v		
r	i	v	e	
r	i	v	e	r

river

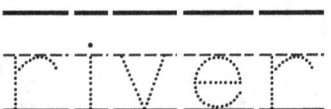

Write the word.

sweet

right

their

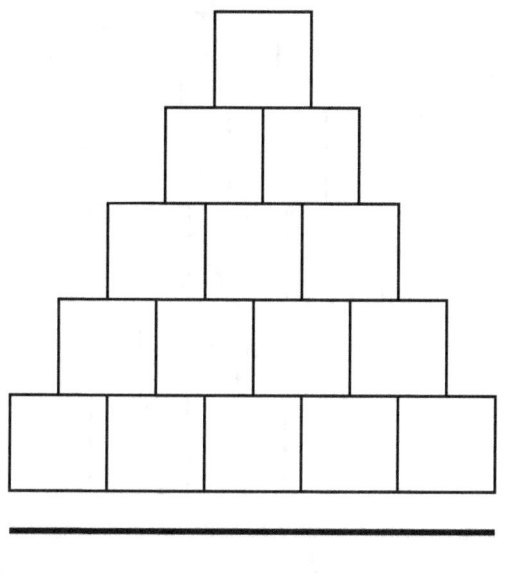

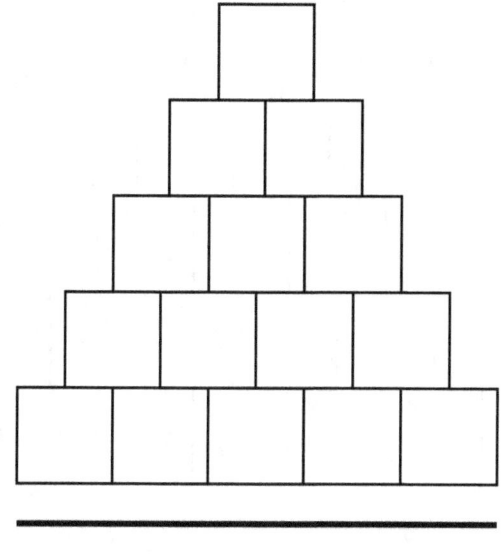

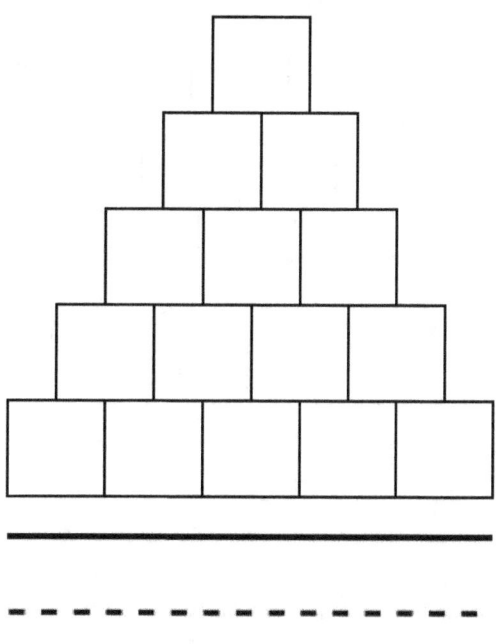

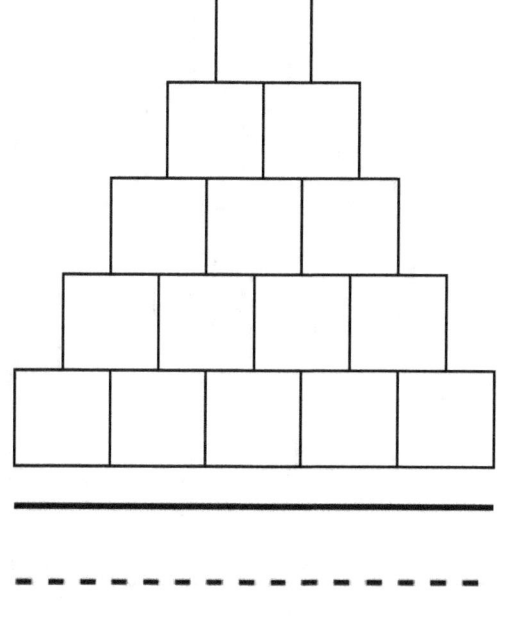

stand

quiet

puppy

mouse

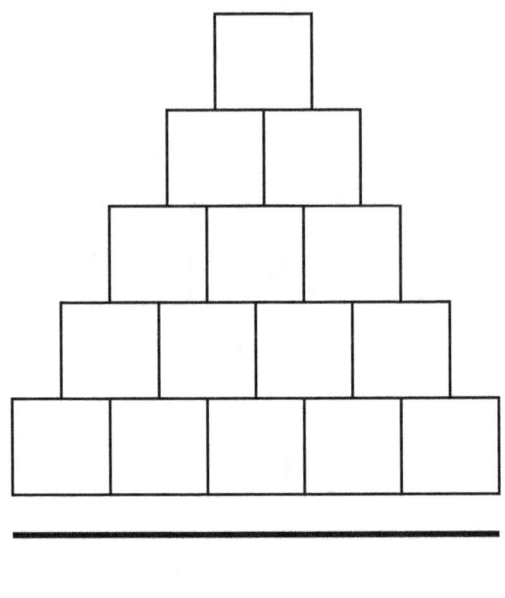

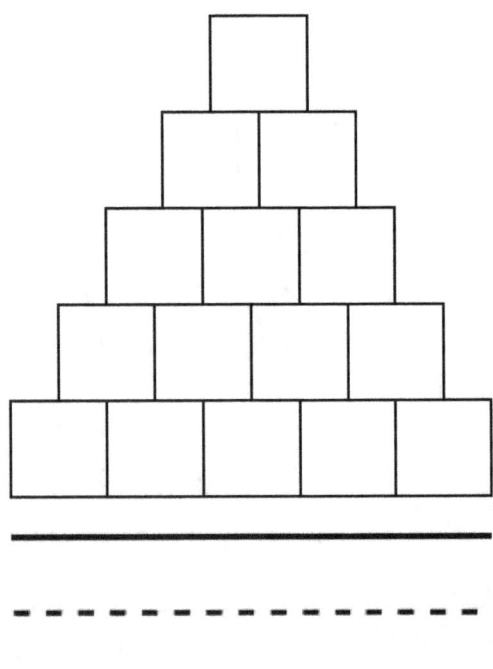

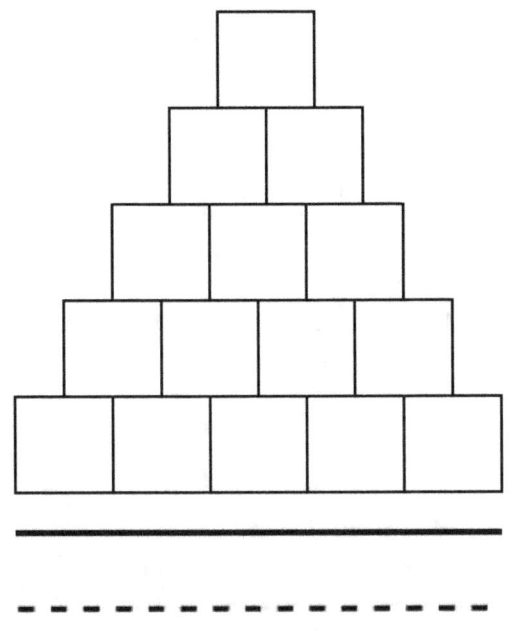

queen

today

women

plant

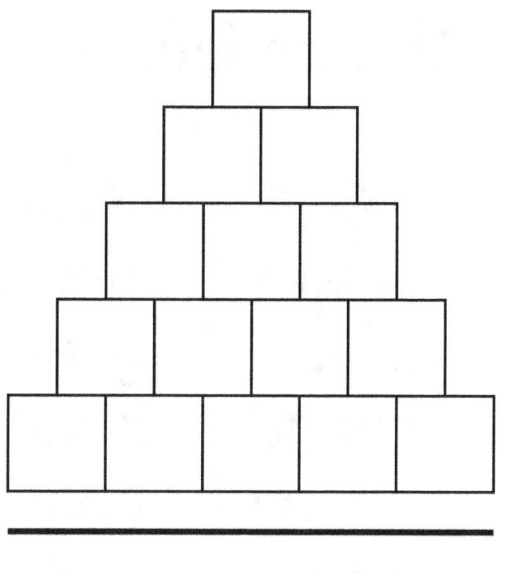

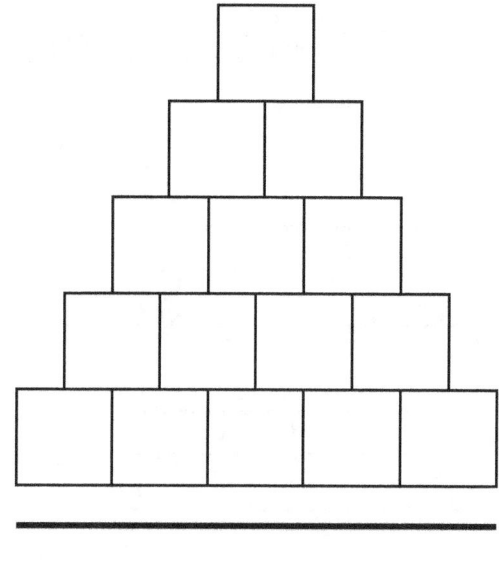

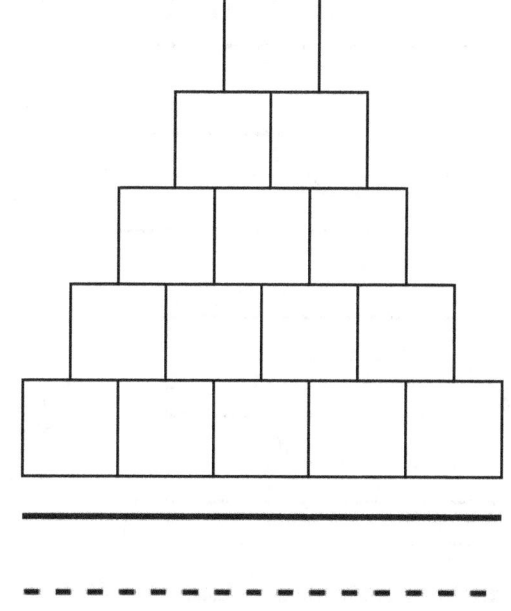

stood

Let's put these
5-letter words in ABC order.

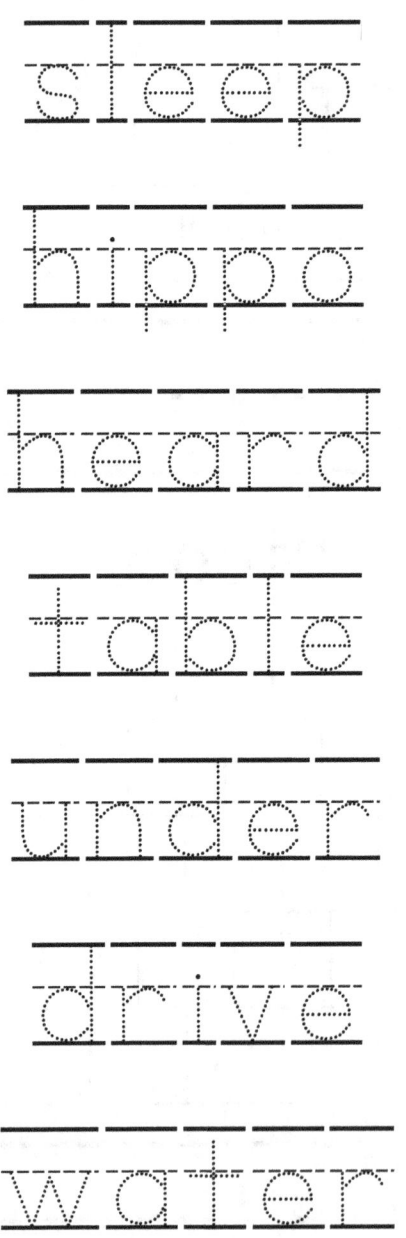

sleep
hippo
heard
table
under
drive
water

again
hippo
close
found
happy
money
horse
juice
lucky
koala
sleep
great
heard
quack
under
drive
began
zebra
bunny
child
could
water
skunk
table

write	juice	plate	lucky
nurse	child	water	
black	stand		
store	woman		
puppy	music		
apple	three		

Circle each spelling word one time in the word search.

c	k	c	b	m	c	h	i	l	d
l	u	c	k	y	s	t	a	n	d
d	n	m	u	s	i	c	l	y	g
w	o	m	a	n	v	x	k	y	b
k	v	r	a	p	p	l	e	k	k
p	l	a	t	e	b	l	a	c	k
j	u	i	c	e	n	u	r	s	e
x	r	s	t	o	r	e	m	z	v
w	r	i	t	e	w	a	t	e	r
p	u	p	p	y	t	h	r	e	e

Use the word bank words
to write them in the correct boxes.

Word Bank

round under sheep

quiet candy party

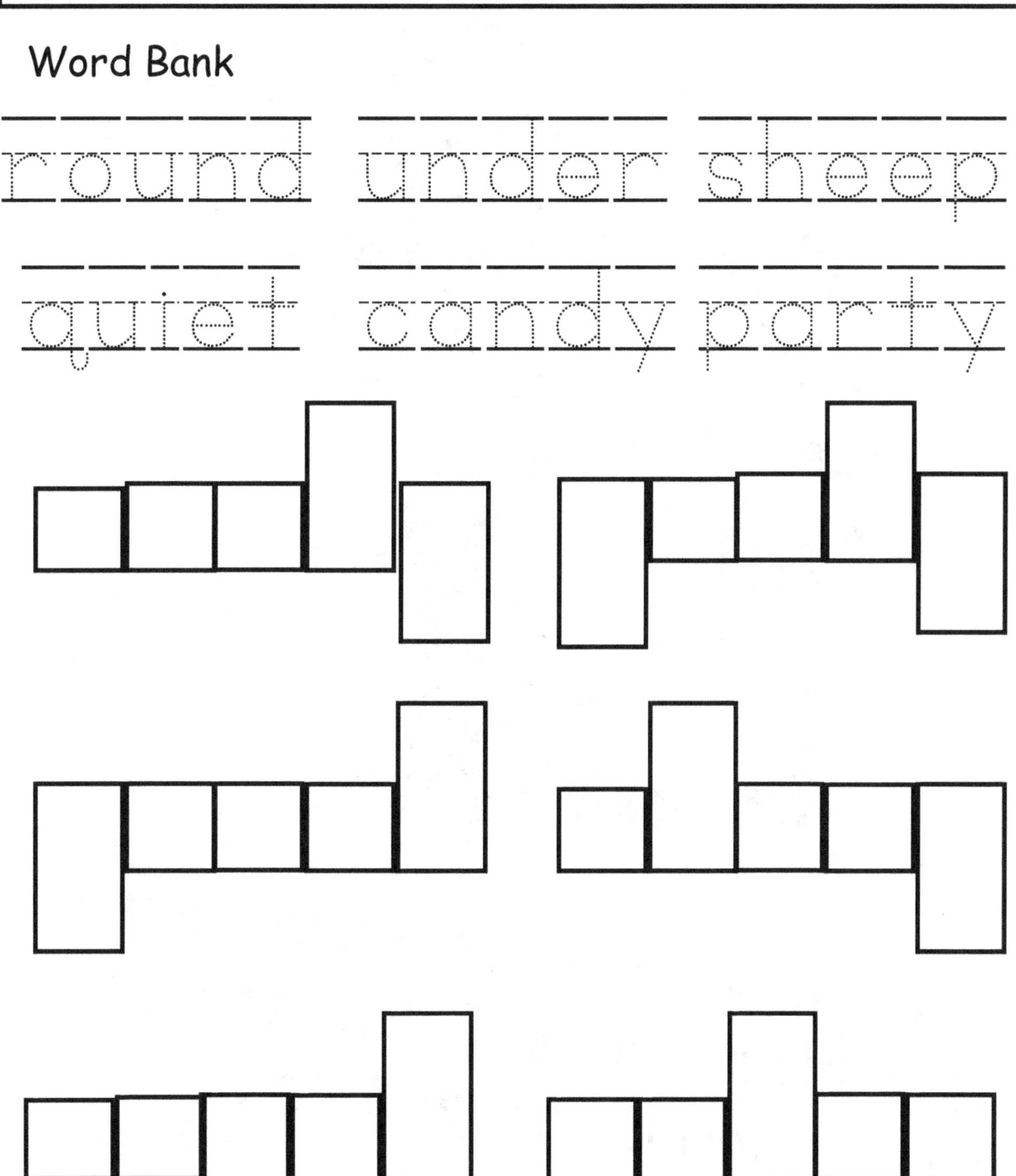

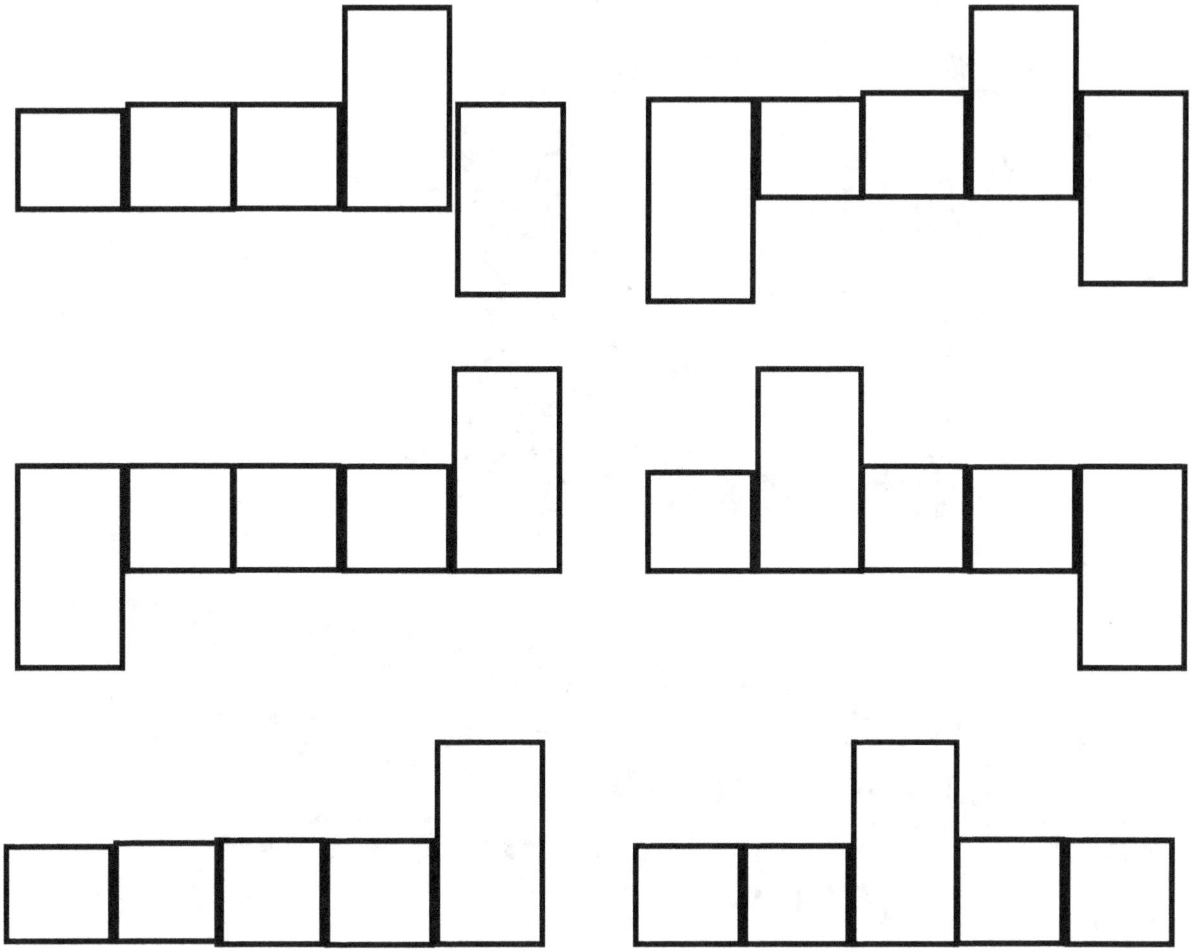

More spelling words to learn.
6-letter words, 7-letter words,
and 8-letter words.

6-Letter Words

Africa
almost
always
animal
answer
before
better
church
circle
coming
cookie
crayon
donkey
Easter
family
farmer
father
flower
splash
freely
garden
golden
health
sister
kitten
little
making
monkey
mother
number
orange
people
please
purple
rabbit
friend
school
spider
sticky
strong
things
turtle
turkey
yellow
zipper
peanut

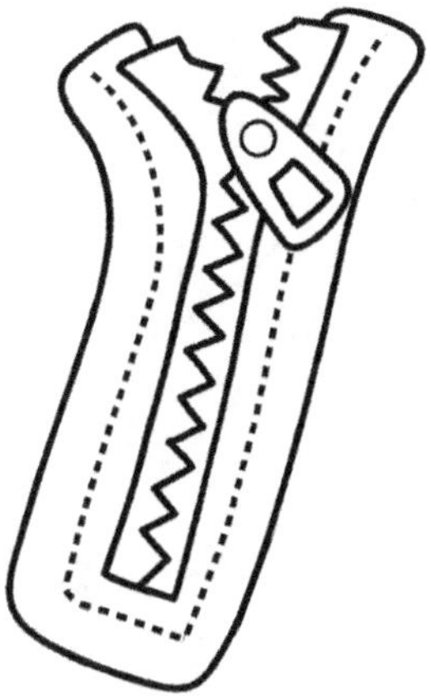

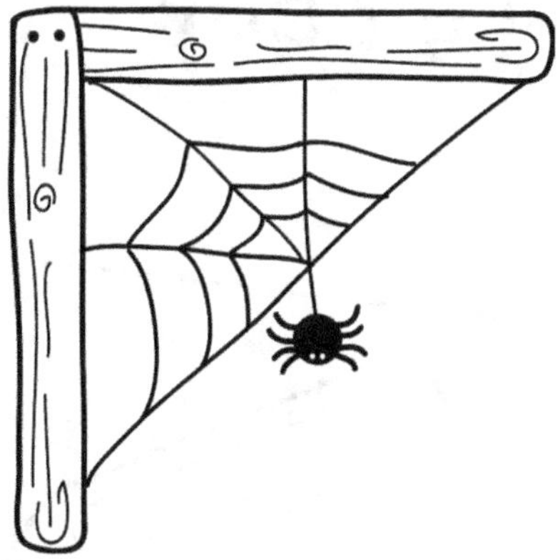

Write your spelling word
one letter at a time.
Follow the example.

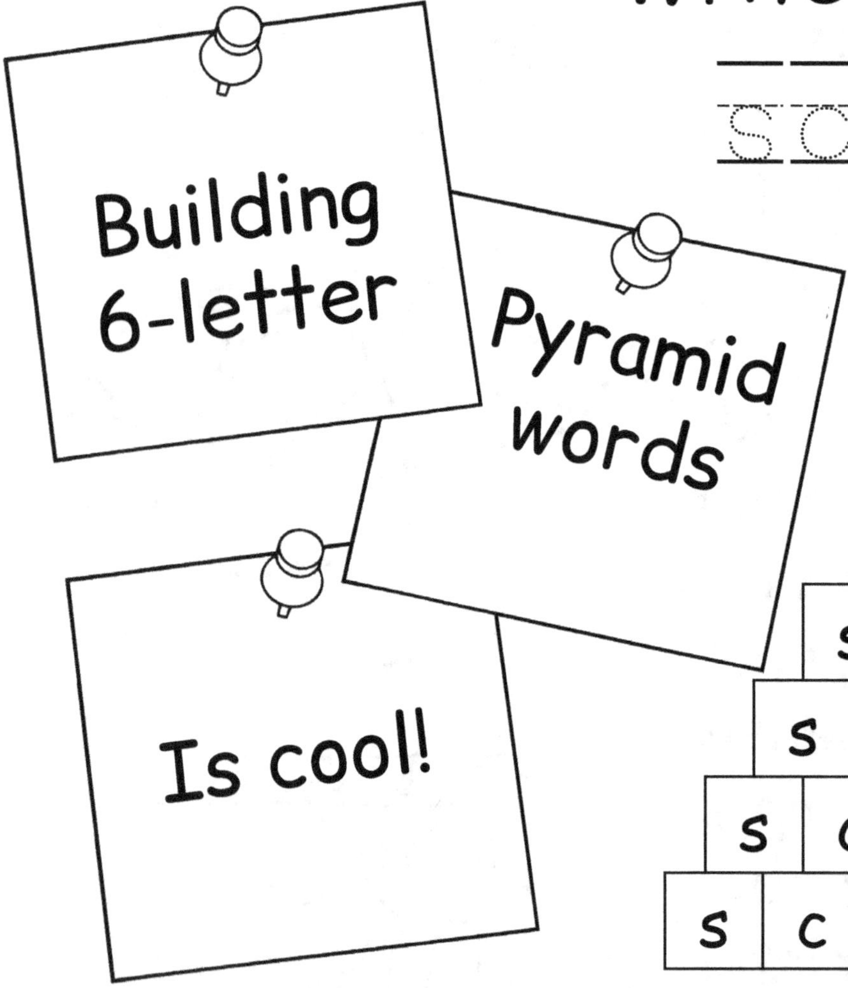
Building
6-letter
Pyramid
words
Is cool!

Write the word.

school

school

s					
s	c				
s	c	h			
s	c	h	o		
s	c	h	o	o	
s	c	h	o	o	l

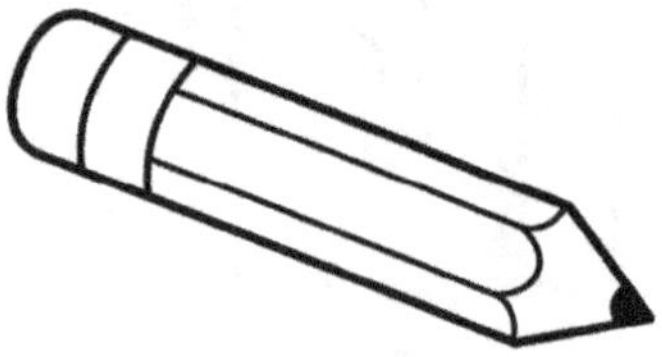

peanut

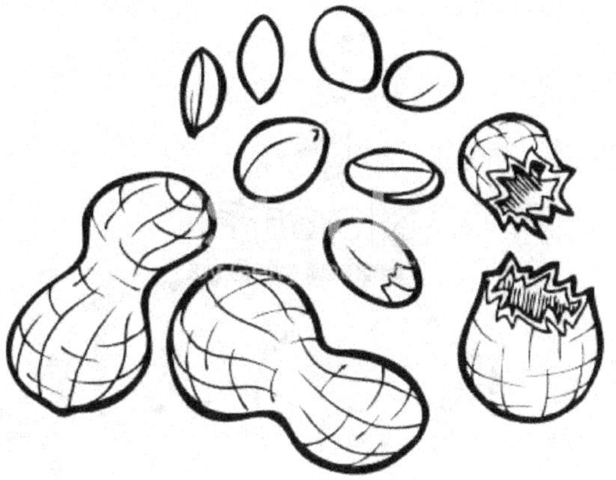

monkey

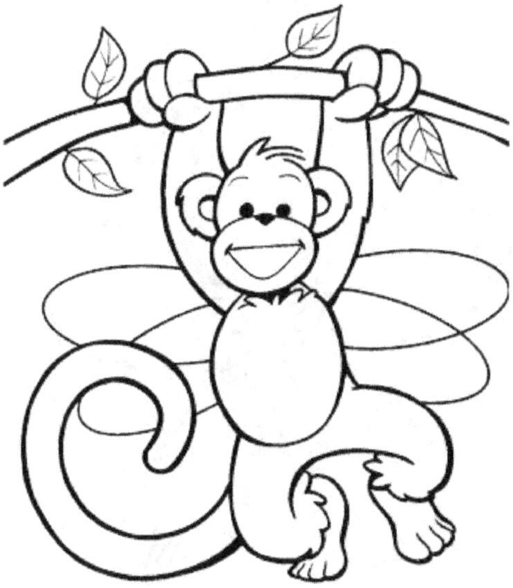

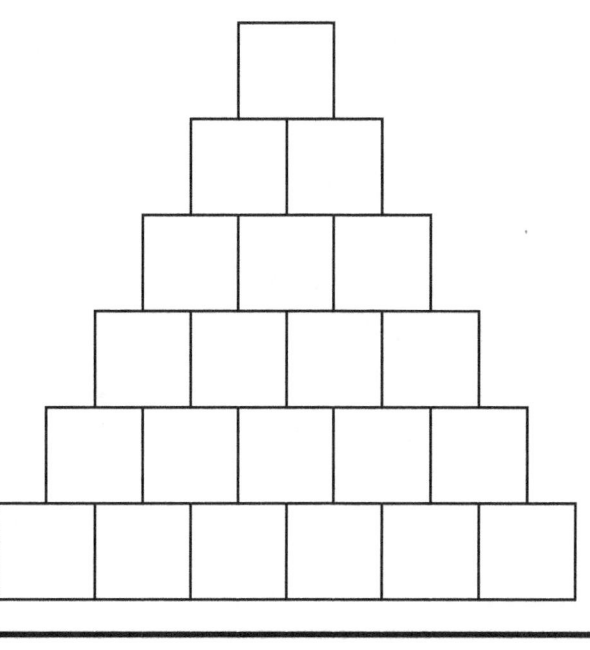

church

flower

Circle each spelling word in the word search.

b	l	d	w	c	o	o	k	i	e
r	a	b	b	i	t	d	m	g	t
t	q	f	a	m	i	l	y	r	t
p	e	o	p	l	e	j	k	y	q
k	e	a	s	t	e	r	p	l	r
q	n	w	s	p	i	d	e	r	c
d	o	n	k	e	y	r	f	j	k
h	m	m	y	e	l	l	o	w	v
g	r	g	k	i	t	t	e	n	p
j	w	f	l	g	a	r	d	e	n

Word Bank

cookie
donkey
easter
garden
kitten
people
rabbit
spider
yellow
family

Add the missing letter. Write the word.

a_imal

ci_le

moth_r

fa_her

ple_se

zi_per

Trace your 7-Letter Words

address
rainbow
because
birthday
chicken
feeling
brother
fireman

giraffe
holiday
picture
present
pumpkin
tractor
Liberia

address
rainbow
because
birthday
chicken

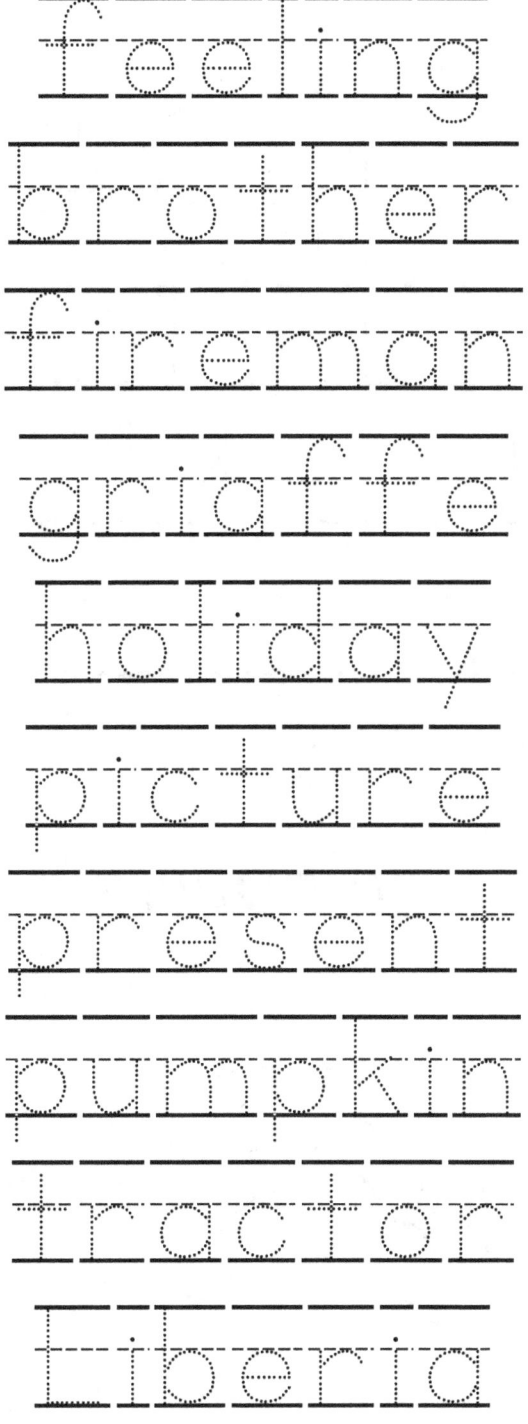

feeling
brother
fireman
griaffe
holiday
picture
present
pumpkin
tractor
Liberia

7-Letter Pyramids

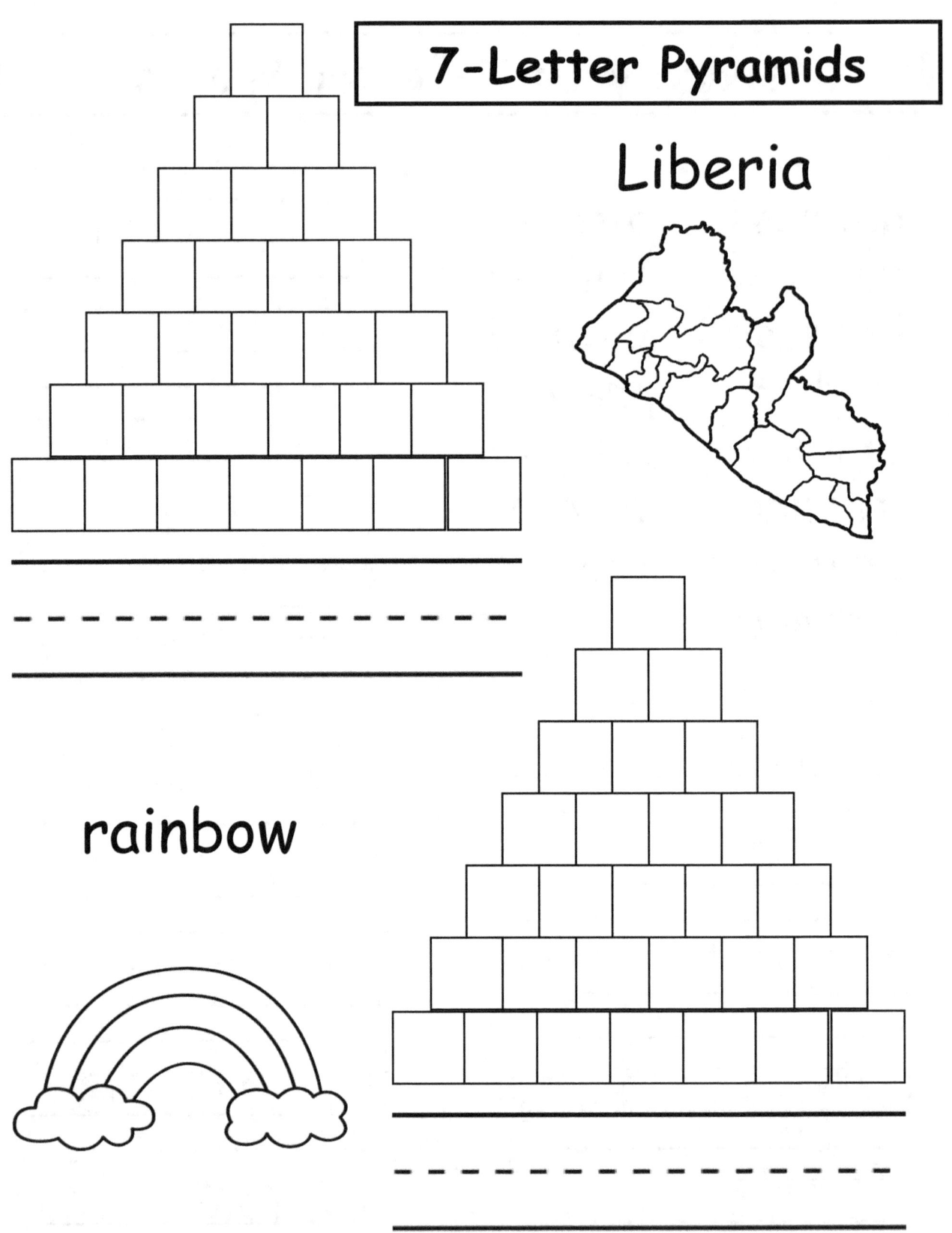

Liberia

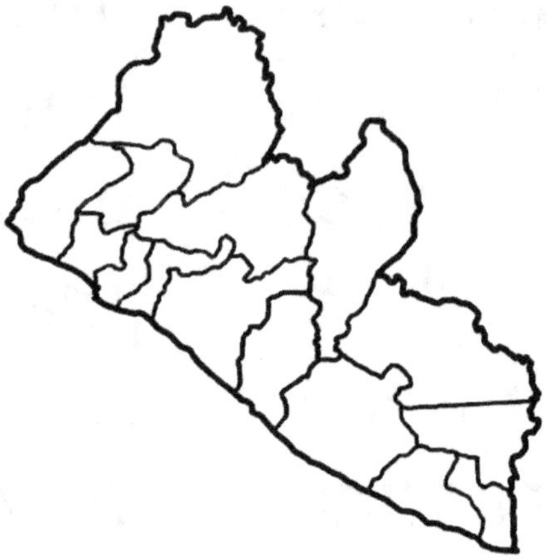

rainbow

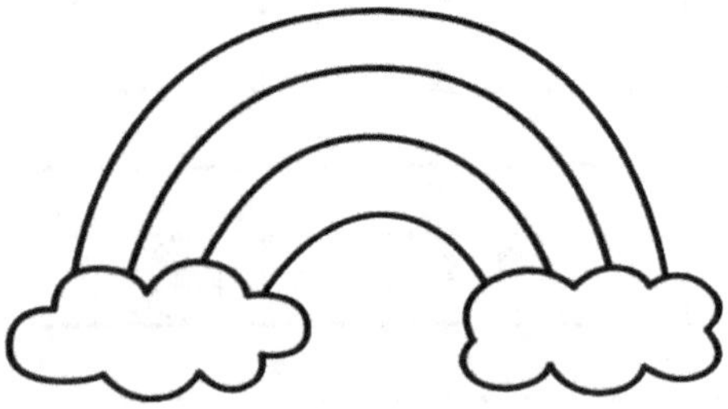

chicken

pumpkin

Trace your 8-Letter Words

Children raindrop
umbrella goldfish
elephant Monrovia
dinosaur

Monrovia dinosaur
children raindrop
umbrella goldfish
elephant

Color Mr. Elephant your favorite color.

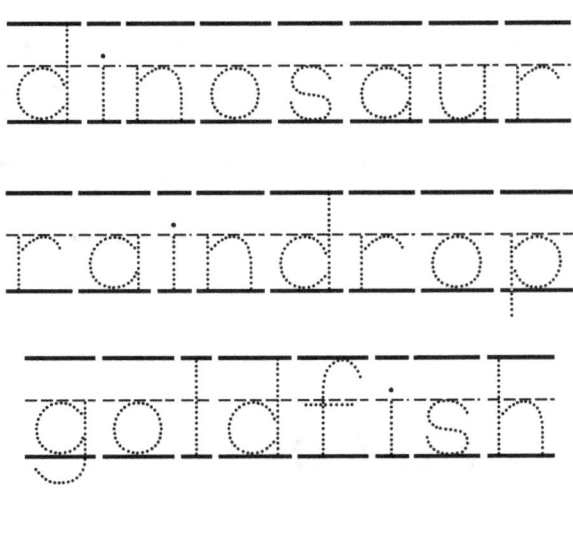

Use the 8-letter words in the correct boxes.

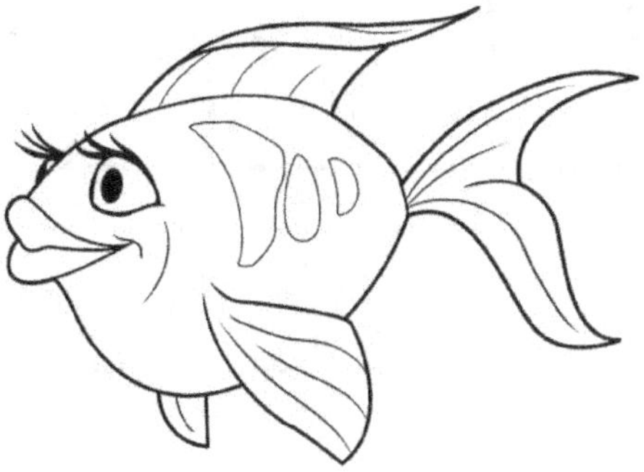

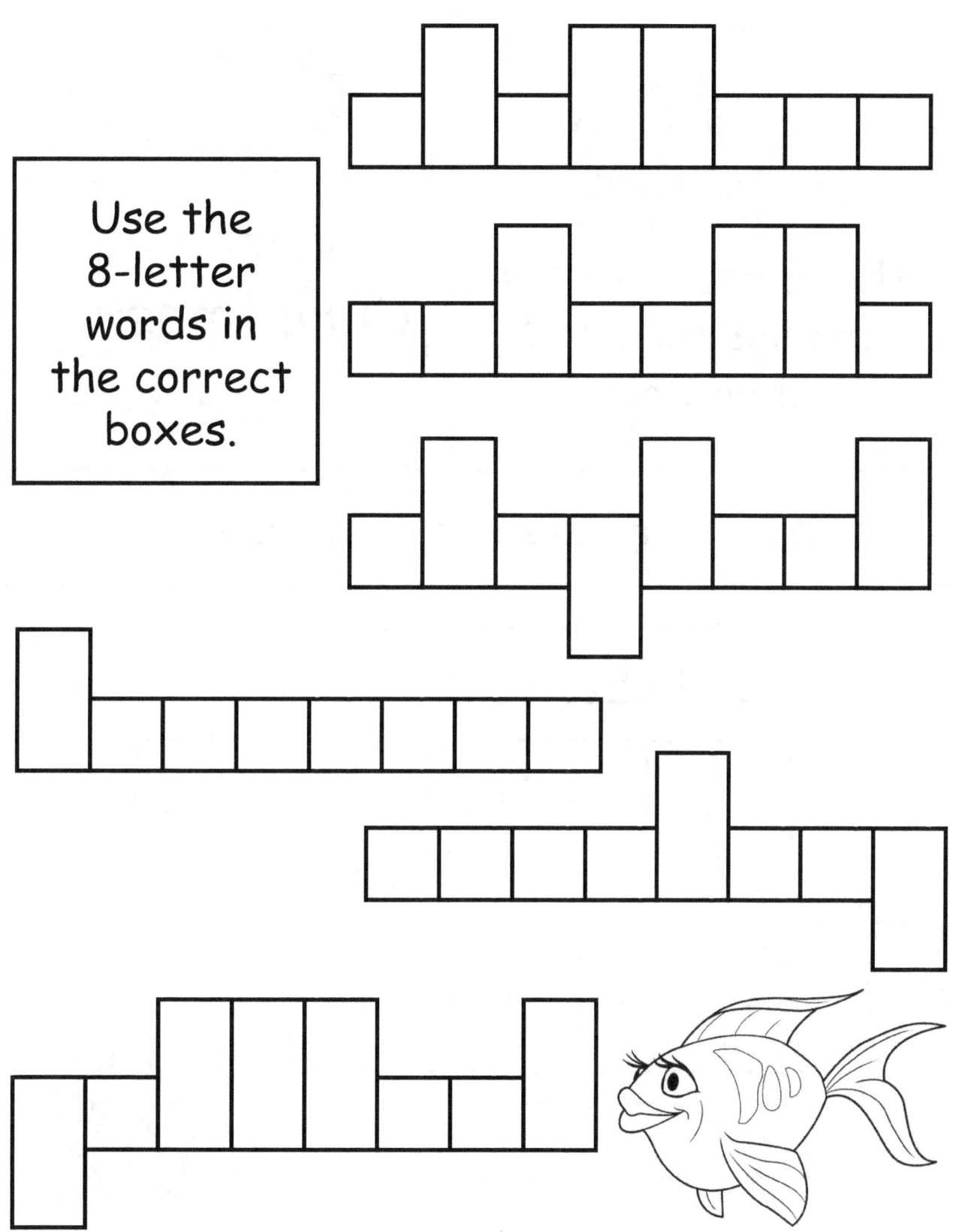

There are 9 letters in pineapple and Christmas.

Write the letters in the correct boxes.

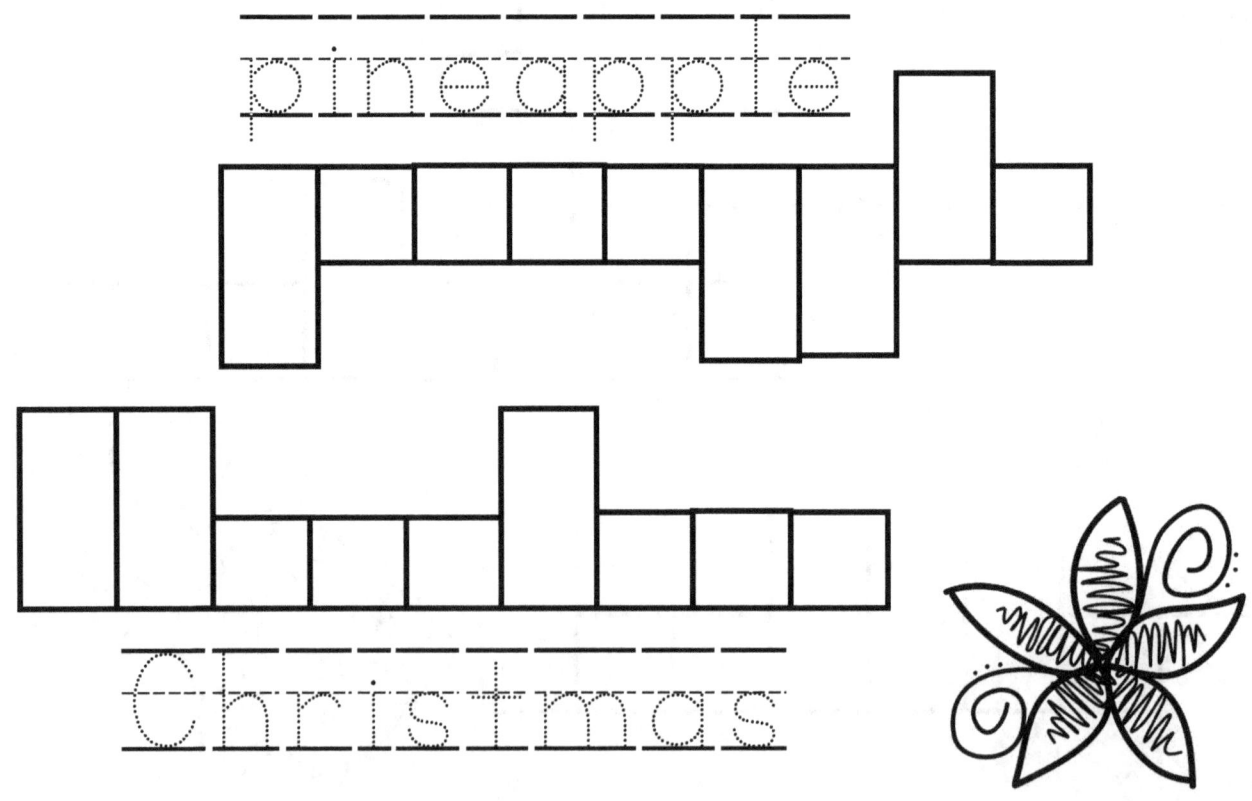

pineapple

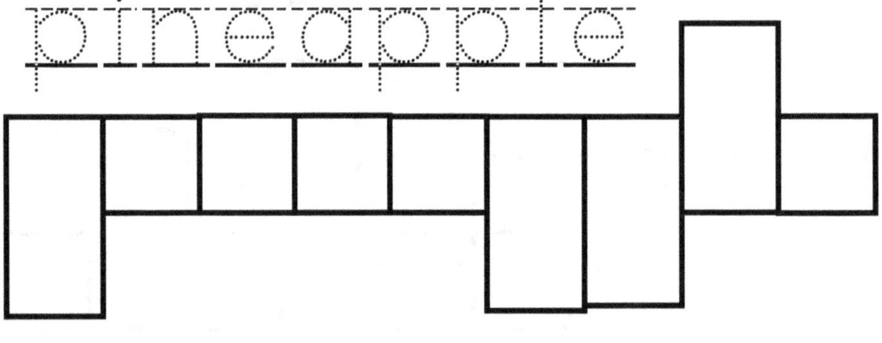

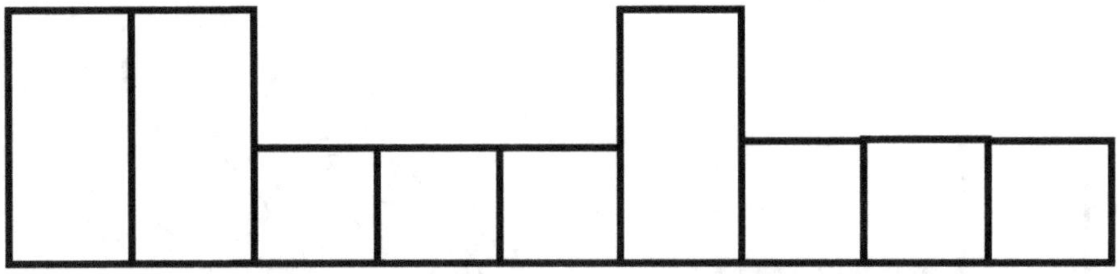

Christmas

Let's Write Some Christmas Words

Jesus

soft drinks

food clothes tree

presents dancers

Santa Claus toys

Number Words

Read it. Trace it. Write it.

0 zero

1 one

2 two

3 three

4 four

5 five

6 six

7 seven

8 eight

9 nine

10 ten

Color Words

Read it. Trace it. Write it. Color it.

blue blue 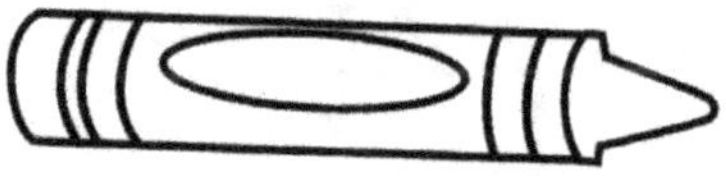

red red 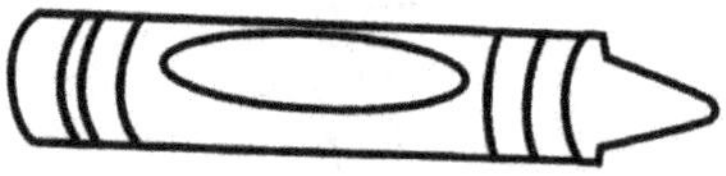

black 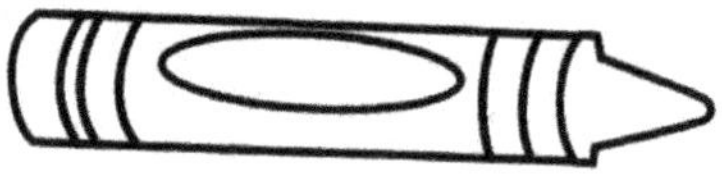

black

brown 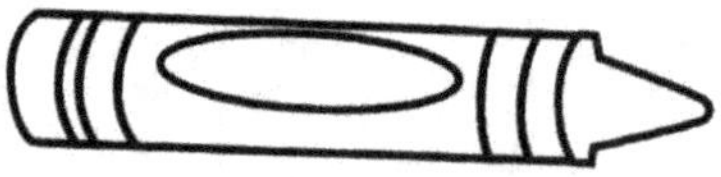

brown

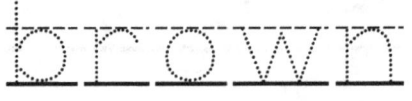

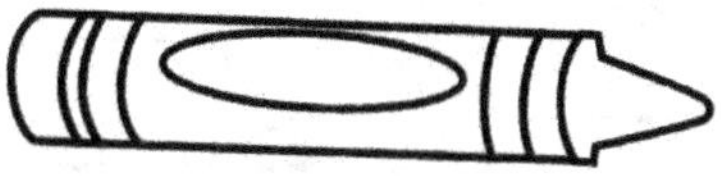

purple

purple

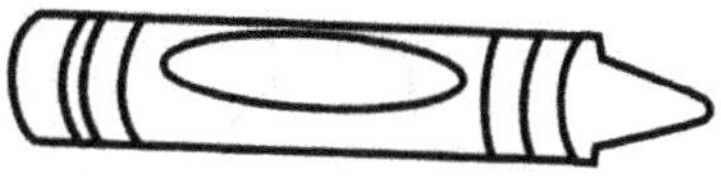

yellow

yellow

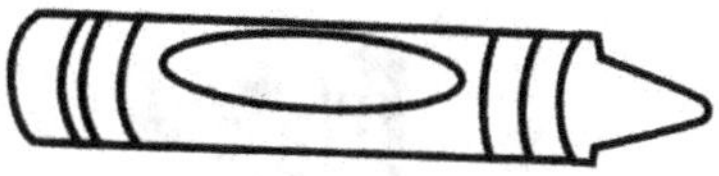

orange

orange

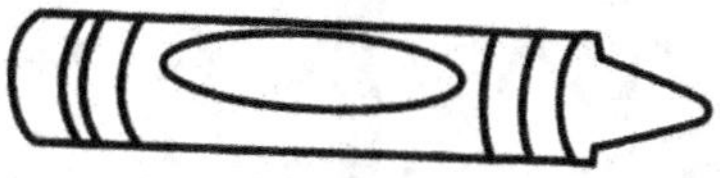

white

white

pink pink

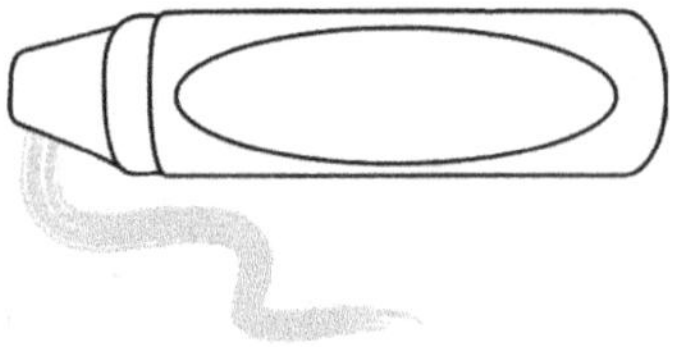

gray gray

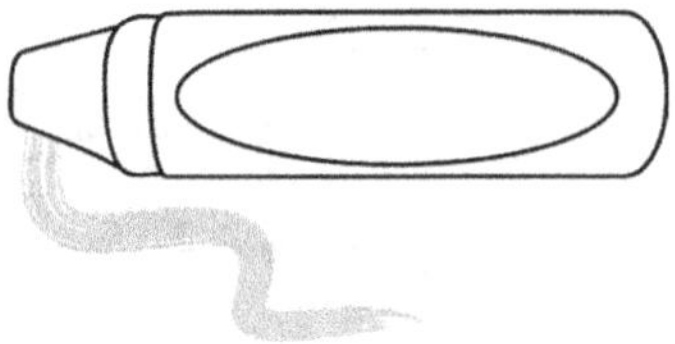

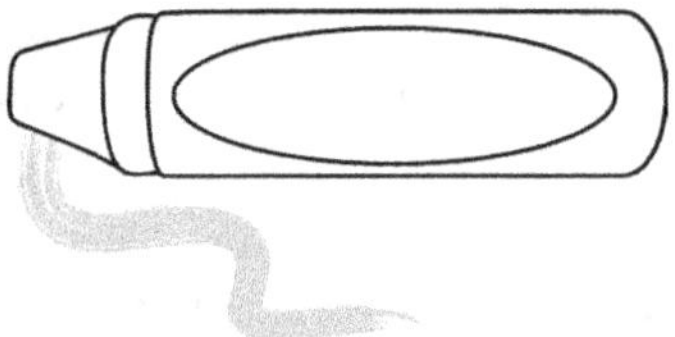

green

green

Color the boat your favorite colors.

Find all the color words in the puzzle.
Circle each one.

n	c	y	e	l	l	o	w	m
b	l	u	e	k	l	m	k	n
o	r	a	n	g	e	r	e	d
p	i	n	k	b	r	o	w	n
r	m	m	v	g	r	a	y	w
b	p	u	r	p	l	e	y	y
f	j	w	h	i	t	e	q	n
k	c	r	b	l	a	c	k	m
z	g	r	e	e	n	n	t	n

My Color Words

Read the color words.
Color the pictures that color.

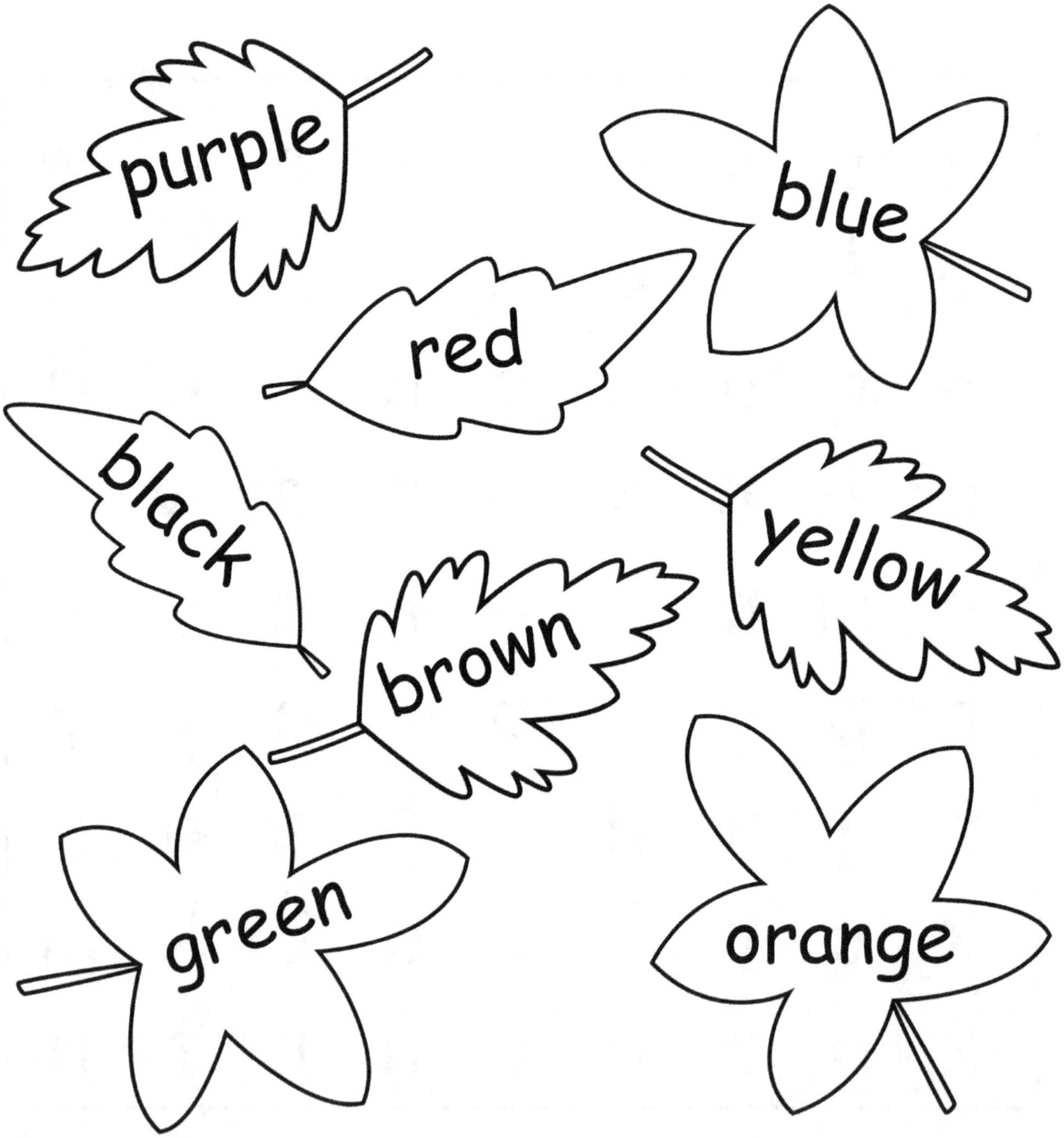

I love
Liberia!

Patriotic Words

Liberia

flag star

stripes

Lone Star vote

red white blue

Rainy Season

puddle
boots
umbrella
raindrop
mud

splash
rainbow
rain
cloud

Circle each spelling word in the word search.

t	v	p	u	d	d	l	e
m	u	d	c	l	o	u	d
u	m	b	r	e	l	l	a
v	r	a	i	n	t	r	l
r	a	i	n	d	r	o	p
m	r	a	i	n	b	o	w
f	b	o	o	t	s	b	x
n	s	p	l	a	s	h	r

Social Relations

Trace the words.
Find the words in the word search.
Circle them.

grandma mother

grandpa father

aunt sister

uncle brother

girl cousin

boy friend

grandma	girl	brother
aunt	grandpa	father
uncle	mother	cousin
boy	sister	friend

c	f	s	i	s	t	e	r	t	k
k	b	o	y	f	a	t	h	e	r
g	r	a	n	d	m	a	d	q	v
f	r	m	f	r	i	e	n	d	q
j	n	m	c	o	u	s	i	n	m
p	c	g	n	g	i	r	l	p	g
h	d	q	b	r	o	t	h	e	r
a	u	n	t	f	u	n	c	l	e
m	k	f	m	o	t	h	e	r	t
g	r	a	n	d	p	a	l	j	r

Fruits & Vegetables

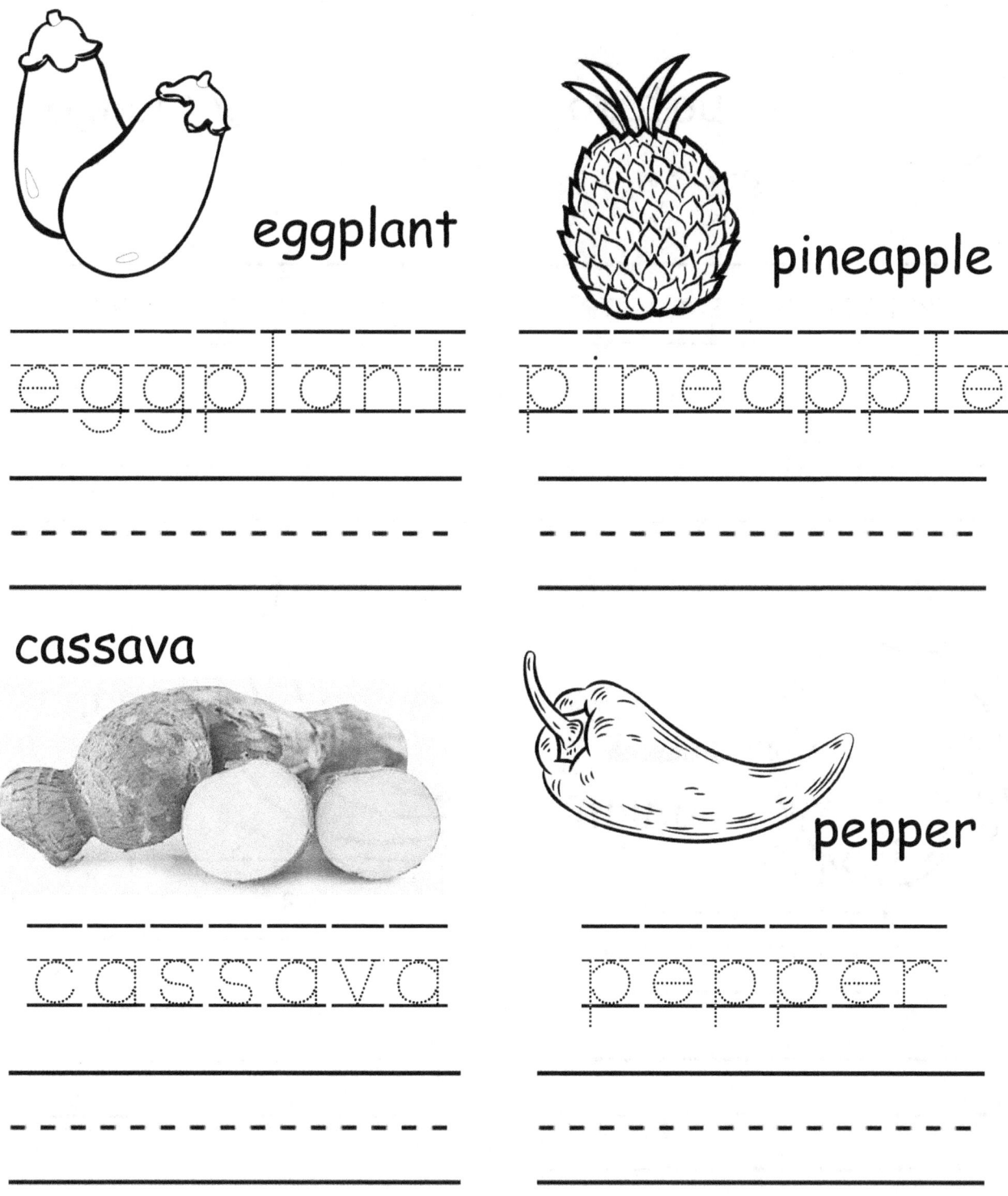

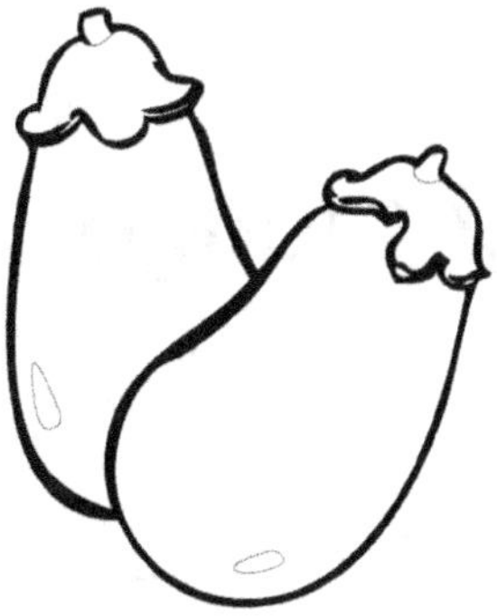

eggplant

pineapple

eggplant

pineapple

cassava

pepper

cassava

pepper

potato

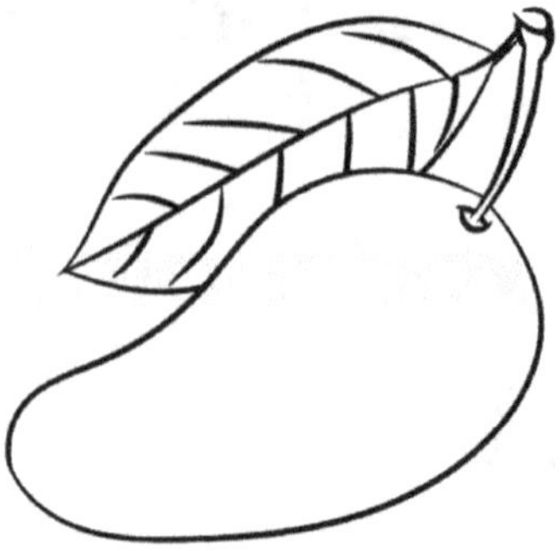

mango

potato

mango

onion

banana

banana

onion

tomato

tomato

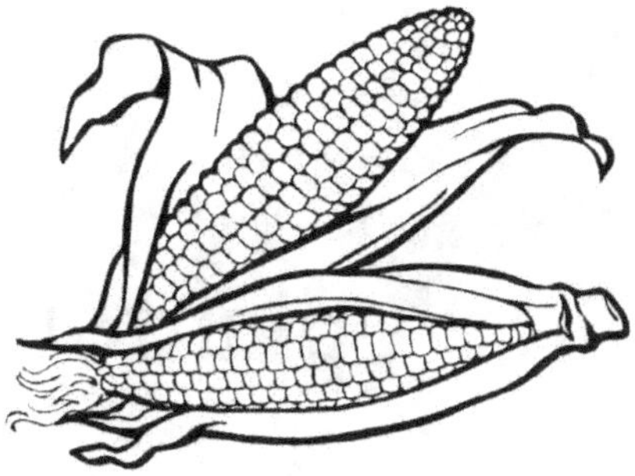

corn

corn

orange

orange

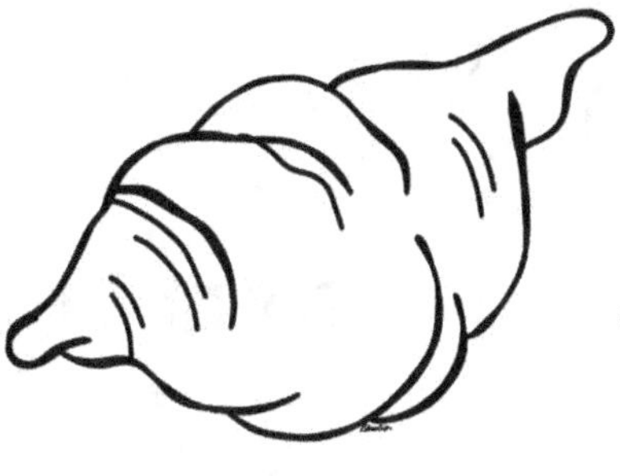

yam

yam

plantain

plantain

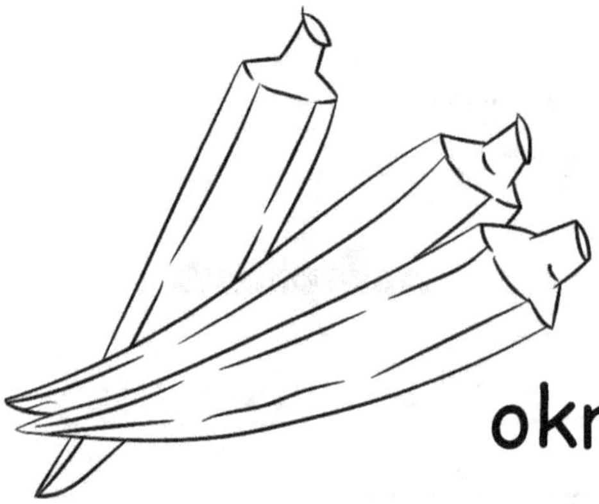

okra

okra

tomato

tomato

What about nuts?

Here Are Some Nuts

peanut

palm nut

peanut

corn

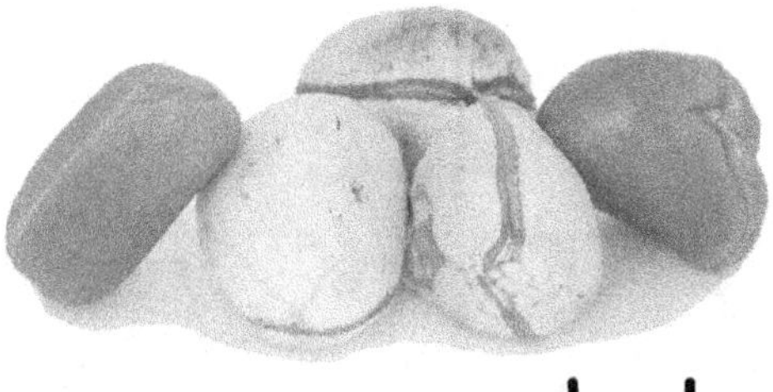

kola nut

coconut

kola nut

coconut

Things At The Beach

sunglasses
boat
canoe
anchor
crab
fish
octopus
sand

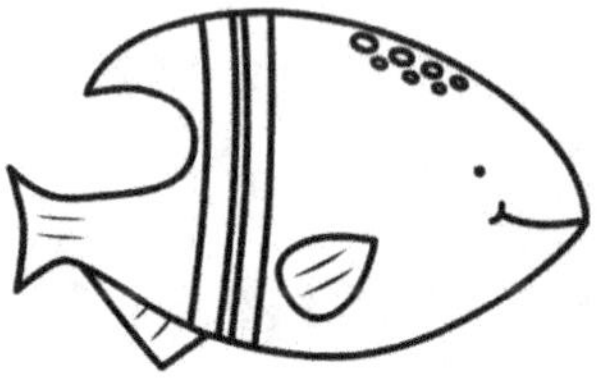

t	n	b	m	k	p	m	k	b	p
k	h	w	a	n	c	h	o	r	c
h	s	a	n	d	w	n	k	z	r
b	m	h	o	c	t	o	p	u	s
r	q	v	c	a	n	o	e	z	r
b	o	a	t	n	f	i	s	h	p
n	r	w	m	w	t	r	q	p	m
c	r	a	b	m	d	h	l	t	b
s	u	n	g	l	a	s	s	e	s
c	b	y	j	z	q	d	y	t	j

Weather Words

Trace the word.

Write the word 2 times

lightning

rainbow

rain

sun

cloud

Read each body word. Trace it, then draw a line to Zaq's body part that matches.

Body Parts

eye	leg
eye	leg
neck	hand
neck	hand
hair	head
hair	head
ear	foot
ear	foot
nose	arm
nose	arm
mouth	belly
mouth	belly

Opposite

young

old

small

big

hot

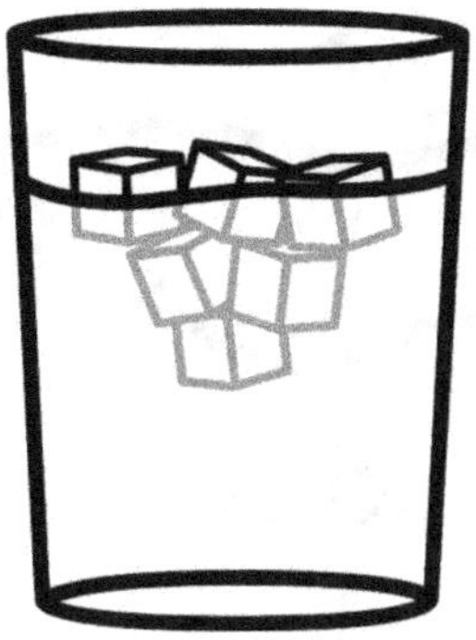

cold

light

heavy

girl

boy

Opposite

wet

dry

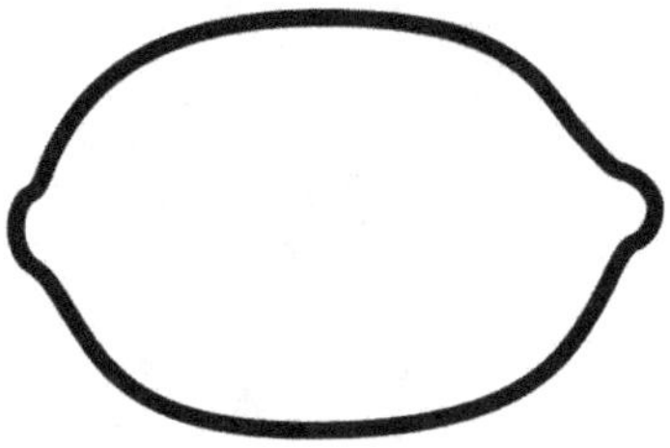

sour

night

day

sweet

asleep

awake

long

short

coat
glasses
pants
shirt
sock
bow

Clothing Words

Find all items in the word search and circle them.

belt
shoe
skirt
lappa
hat
headtie

g	v	b	l	a	p	p	a	t
t	s	k	i	r	t	k	k	j
l	c	z	s	h	o	e	c	f
v	n	c	x	s	h	i	r	t
s	o	c	k	b	e	l	t	t
p	g	l	a	s	s	e	s	y
h	e	a	d	t	i	e	n	n
c	o	a	t	h	a	t	n	p
b	o	w	p	a	n	t	s	d

Let's Eat

Read each word, then draw a line to the object that matches.

plate

cup

bowl

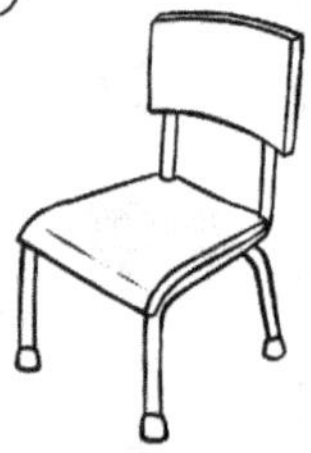

glass

fork

chair

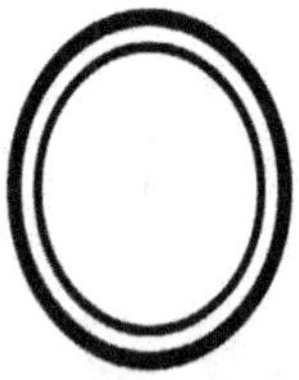

spoon

Read each word, then draw a line to the object that matches.

gift candle hat cake bag

ice cream game ballon candy

HAPPY BIRTHDAY

to

____

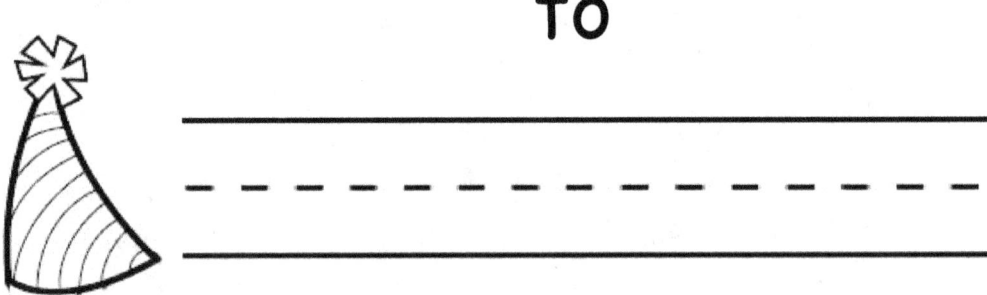

My birthday is

____

Months Of The Year

July
26!

January

February

March

April

May

June

July

August

September

October

November

December

December
25th

January
February
March
April
May
June

Can you find the months in the puzzle?

July
August
September
October
November
December

l	g	j	l	M	a	y	k	c	h	b
S	e	p	t	e	m	b	e	r	z	z
n	p	r	t	J	a	n	u	a	r	y
O	c	t	o	b	e	r	z	j	y	l
m	J	u	l	y	t	A	p	r	i	l
y	r	D	e	c	e	m	b	e	r	l
F	e	b	r	u	a	r	y	w	j	q
n	v	N	o	v	e	m	b	e	r	n
n	r	q	A	u	g	u	s	t	z	x
k	v	b	r	v	n	m	v	l	k	c
M	a	r	c	h	y	r	J	u	n	e

7 Days A Week

Days of the week must start with a capital or uppercase letter.

Trace it.

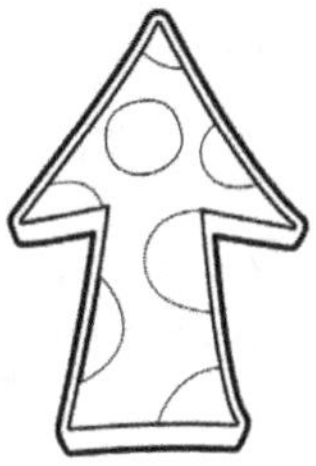

Box it.

Write it.

Sunday

Sunday

Monday

Monday

Tuesday

Tuesday

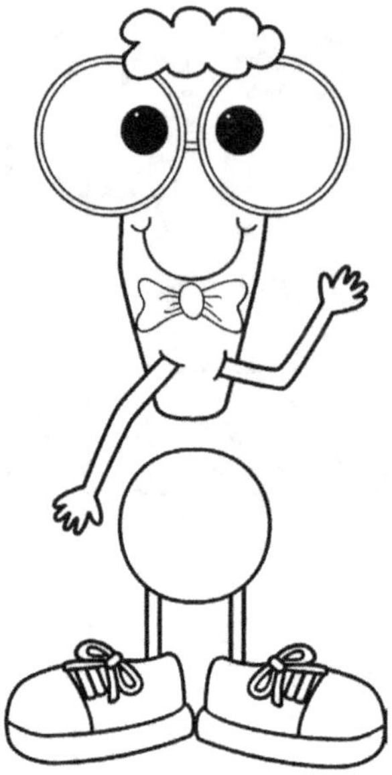

Wednesday

Wednesday

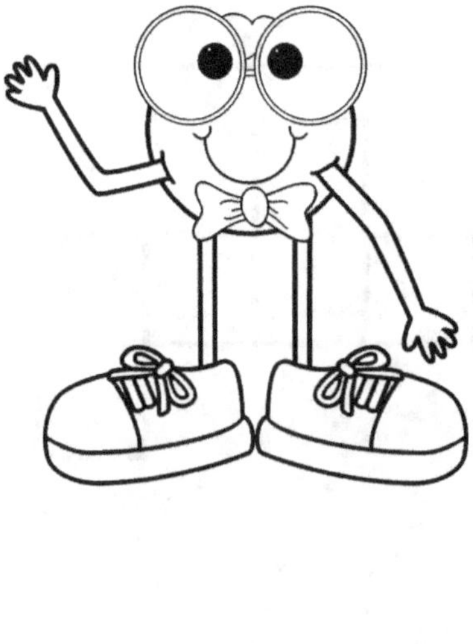

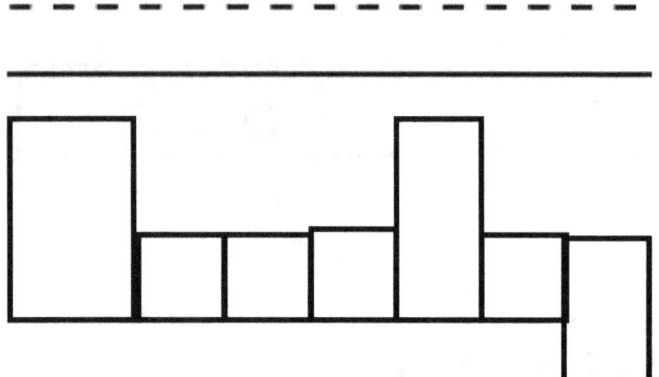

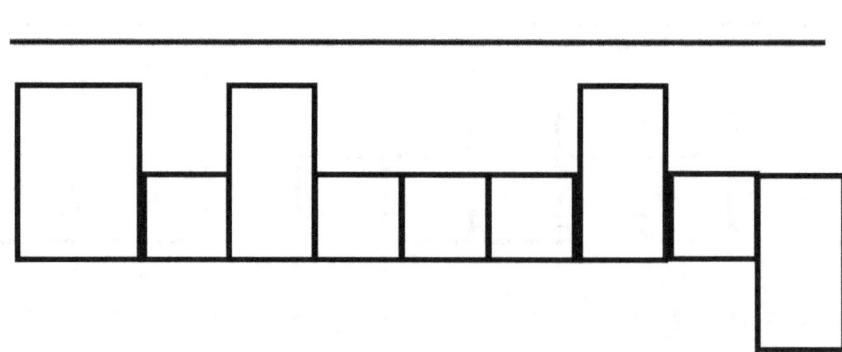

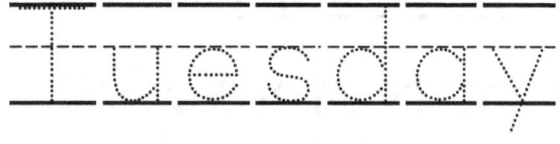

Thursday

Thursday

Friday

Friday

Weekend Days

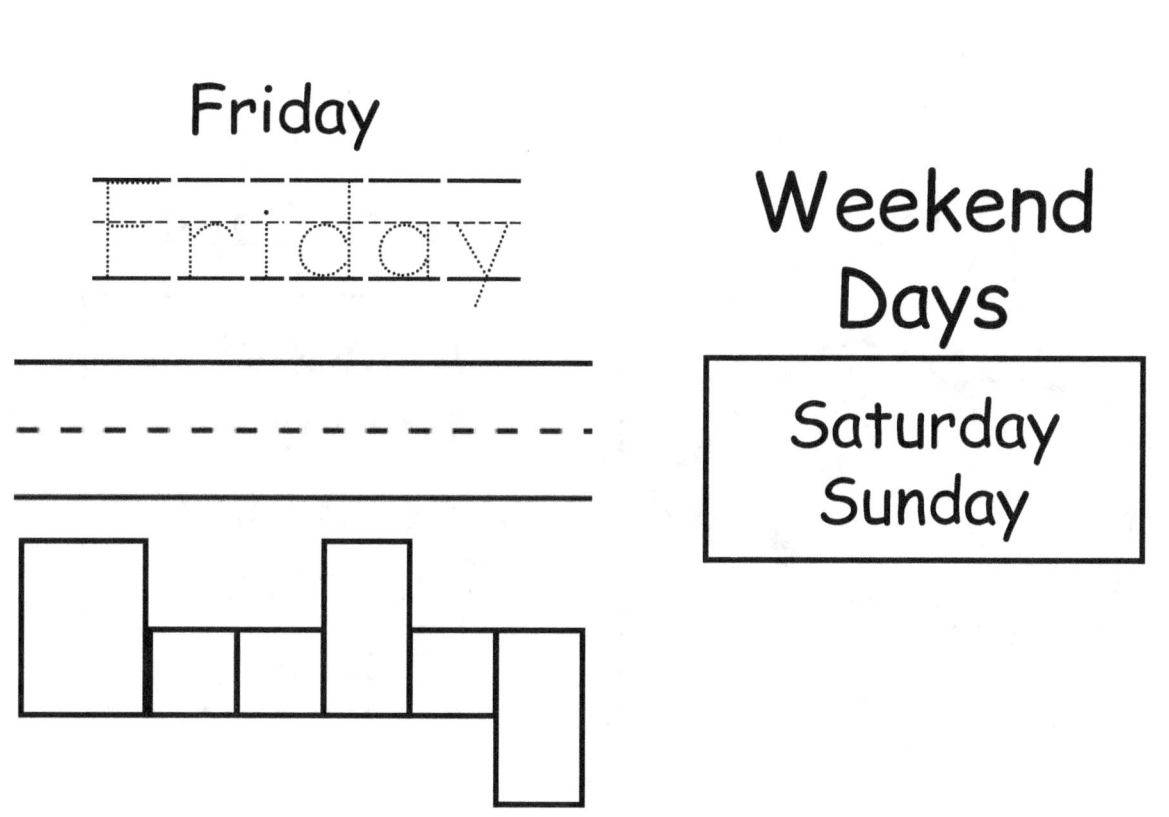

Saturday
Sunday

Saturday

Saturday

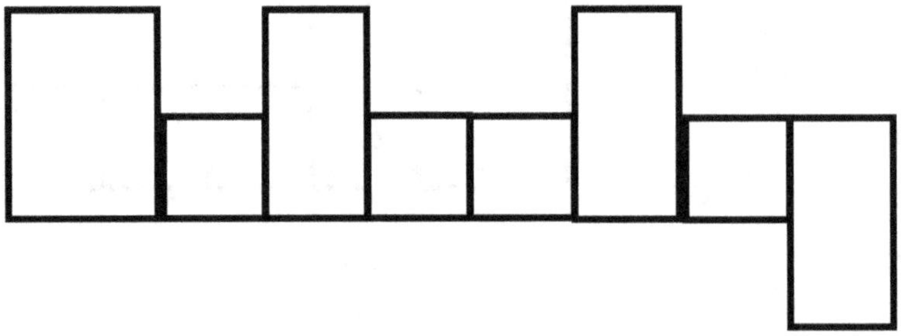

School Days

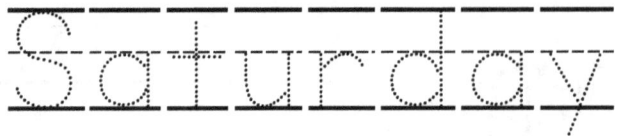

Monday
Tuesday
Wednesday
Thursday
Friday

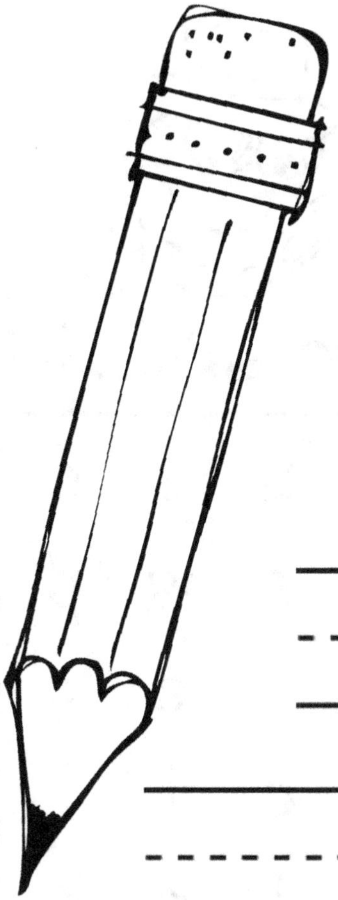

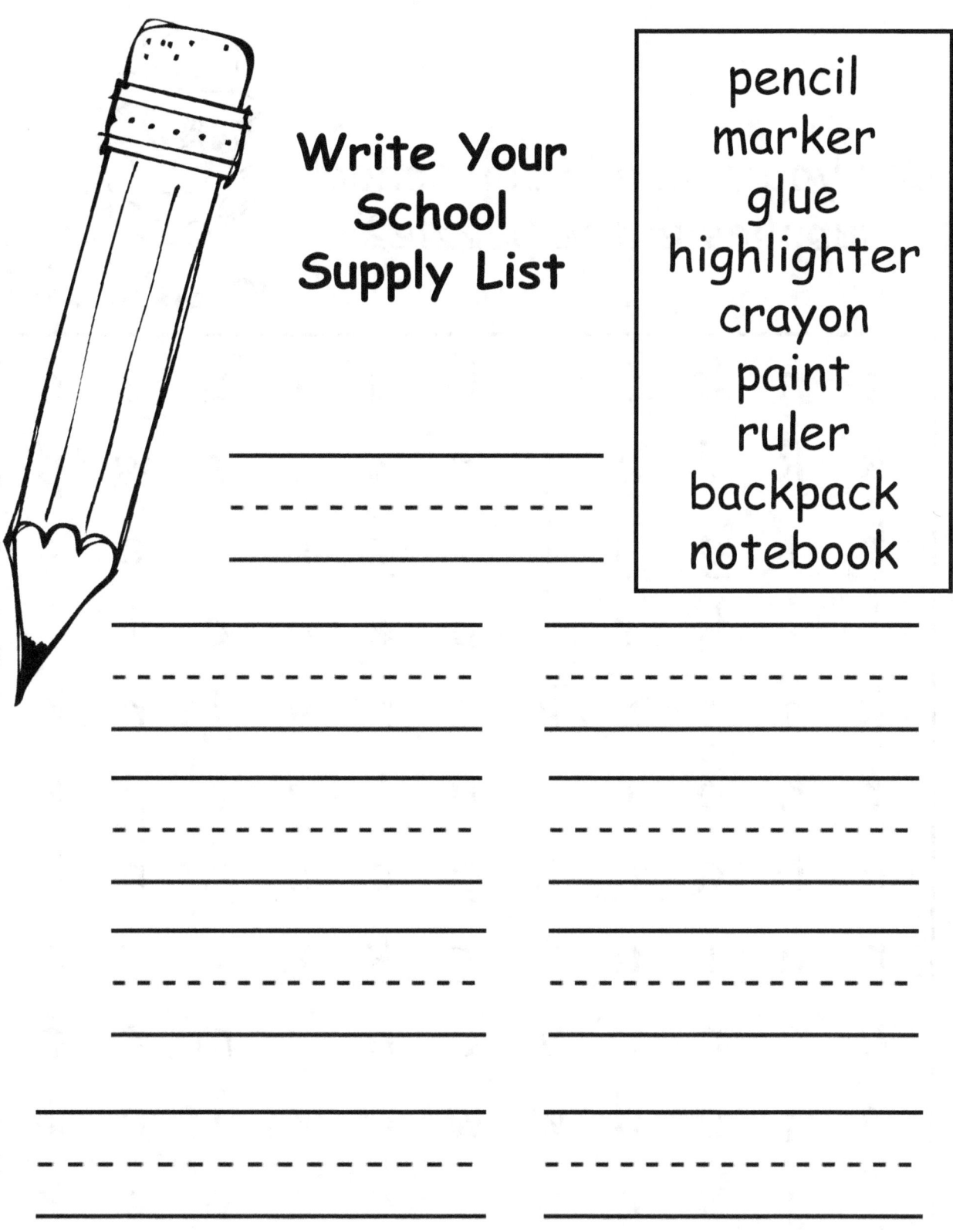

Write Your School Supply List

pencil
marker
glue
highlighter
crayon
paint
ruler
backpack
notebook

Can you find all your school supplies in the puzzle?

z	n	k	f	t	b	g	l	u	e	c
k	k	f	b	j	r	w	c	n	w	p
h	i	g	h	l	i	g	h	t	e	r
l	l	k	t	c	p	e	n	c	i	l
k	m	a	r	k	e	r	y	l	n	n
f	n	b	l	r	u	l	e	r	z	k
r	b	a	c	k	p	a	c	k	r	b
p	a	i	n	t	r	k	x	v	v	n
q	c	r	a	y	o	n	y	m	c	f
n	j	r	d	w	w	r	k	t	r	l
j	j	x	n	o	t	e	b	o	o	k

Congratulations!

It's time to celebrate the graduate.

graduate

cupcake

Trace the words, then find them in the word search puzzle.

celebrate dream

camera school

diploma cap gown

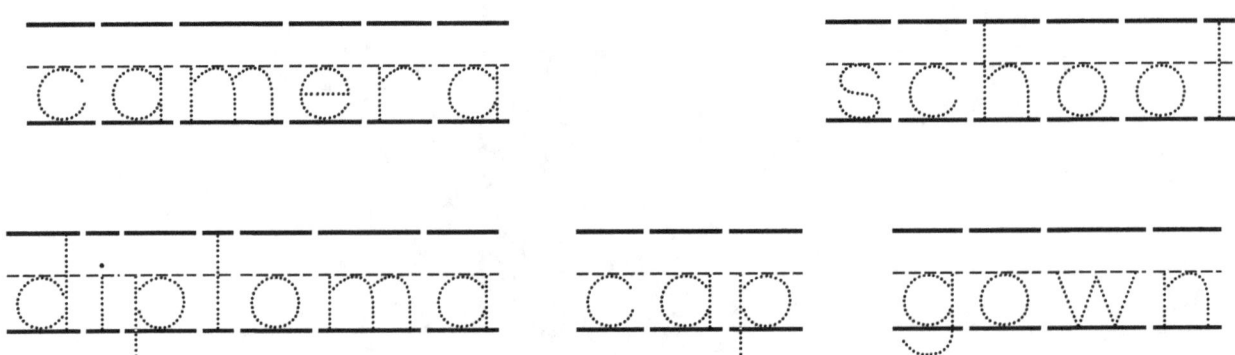

Graduation Words

t	v	c	a	p	b	m	j	t
c	a	m	e	r	a	t	z	x
h	z	r	m	g	o	w	n	m
c	e	l	e	b	r	a	t	e
r	d	i	p	l	o	m	a	l
s	c	h	o	o	l	c	w	r
j	y	c	u	p	c	a	k	e
g	r	a	d	u	a	t	e	c
v	t	m	d	r	e	a	m	g

Kindergarten Spelling List

Two-Letter Words

am	an	by
or	my	us
as	is	we
Mr.	ax	
of	it	
at	Ms.	
be	no	
Dr.	on	
go	do	
me	in	
he	ox	
up	so	
hi	to	
if	TV	

One-Letter Words

a
I

Three-Letter Words

eat	gee	boo	got	she
act	hot	bug	gun	sit
air	pin	buy	her	son
any	out	cab	hey	sun
ate	cry	can	hit	tag
his	wax	cub	how	taz
bad	rob	did	its	the
ban	job	all	jar	was
bat	Mrs.	eel	kid	way
bay	fan	end	lad	who
bed	has	fad	lap	owl
bee	nap	ape	led	few
pat	six	are	lot	zip
top	sky	art	put	you
get	low	ask	ran	old
two	off	fed	rat	egg
use	our	fit	rip	not
pad	pal	fly	run	may
cap	pay	for	saw	dot
him	pop	fur	sea	lit
car	pot	gap	see	toe

pan
new
hay
yea
tap
set
ant
say
wed
one
and
cup
dam
had
day
van
row
ten
hen
leg
now
red
bus
eye
win

zoo
jet
man
pie
sad
yes
ice
cow
oil
try
fun
gum
key
arm
toy
jam
mat
hog
cat
why
cut
mad
wet
but
log

pig
hut
fox
add
let
mug
hat
big
nut
boy
box
ram
hug
shy
ham
dog
bet

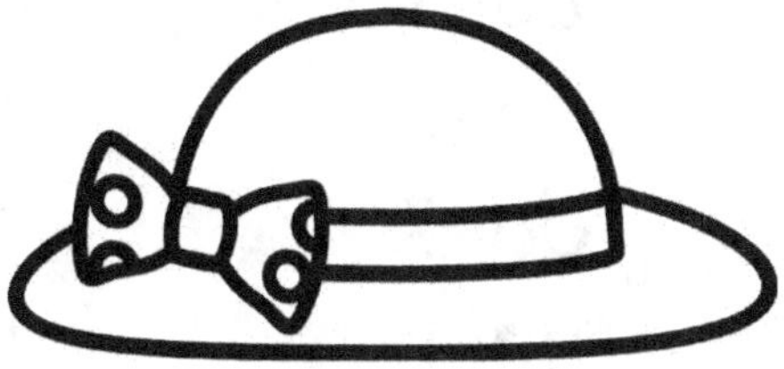

Four-Letter Words

also
away
baby
back
barn
bead
bear
been
beep
bend
bent
best
come
cost
crab
dark
drop
lion
lose
loss
more
move

neat
next
nine
only
open
over
play
read
rent
ride
rule
safe
said
seal
send
shoe

sick
side
soft
some
song
soon
star
stop
sure
tend
than
that
them
then
they
this
week
went
were
will
wish
word

work
worm
yard
your
duck
easy
ever
face
farm
feel
fill
find
fire
fish
foot
four

free
frog
from
game
gave
gift
gold
grow
hair
hand
hard
have
head
hear
hers
high
hill
hole
hope

hurt
jump
keep
kind
kite
king
ring
five
live
miss
kiss
call
tall
mall
wall
ball
fall
talk
walk
good
food
book
look
tell

sell
well
bell
cake
take
bake
down
town
bull
pull
full
name
same
help

Four-Letter Words

calf
here
love
made
many
both
came
used
very
wait
told
girl
give
glad
tree
true
want
wave
lost
meow
pole
poor
with
wolf

meet
lamb
land
city
river
road
room
cold
colt
last
late
lend

yell
zero
what
when
goat
light
like
line
deer

doll
bird
blue
boss
care
palm

rock
sent
pass
door
dove
draw
rice

Five-Letter Words

about
above
after
small
stick
store
story
swim
table
these
thing
three
tiger
train
tried
white
witch
woman
write
zebra
alone
apple

beach
begin
black
bring
brown
camel
candy
carry
clean
color
count
daddy
dream
dress
eight
every
fight
floor
ghost
goose
again
hippo

close
found
happy
money
horse
juice
lucky
koala
sleep
great
heard
quack
under
drive
began
bunny
child
could
water

grass
green
heart
hello
house
large
moose
music
nurse

Five-Letter Words

paper
party
plate
price
round
seven
sheep
skunk
quiet
puppy
mouse
queen

plant
stood
women
today

their
right
sweet
stand

Six-Letter Words

almost
always
animal
answer
before
better
church
circle
coming
cookie
crayon

donkey
Easter
family
farmer
father
flower
splash
freely
garden
golden
health

sister
kitten
little
making
monkey
mother
number
orange
people
please
purple

rabbit
friend
school
spider
sticky
strong

things
turkey
yellow
zipper
Africa
turtle
peanut

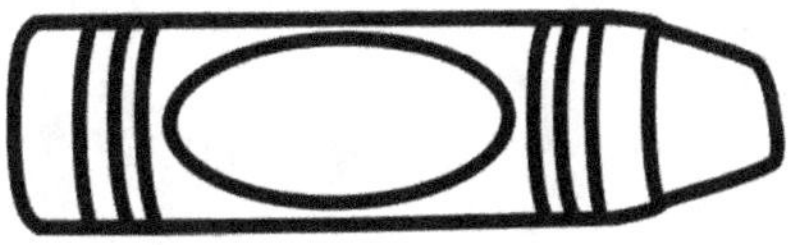

Seven-Letter Words

Address
rainbow
because
birthday
chicken
feeling
brother
fireman
giraffe
holiday
picture
present
pumpkin
tractor
Liberia

Eight-Letter Words

Children
umbrella
elephant
pineapple
dinosaur
raindrop
goldfish
Monrovia

Nine-Letter Words

Christmas

Word Smart Puzzles

Look at the pictures and idenitify the objects by filling in the crossword puzzles across and down.

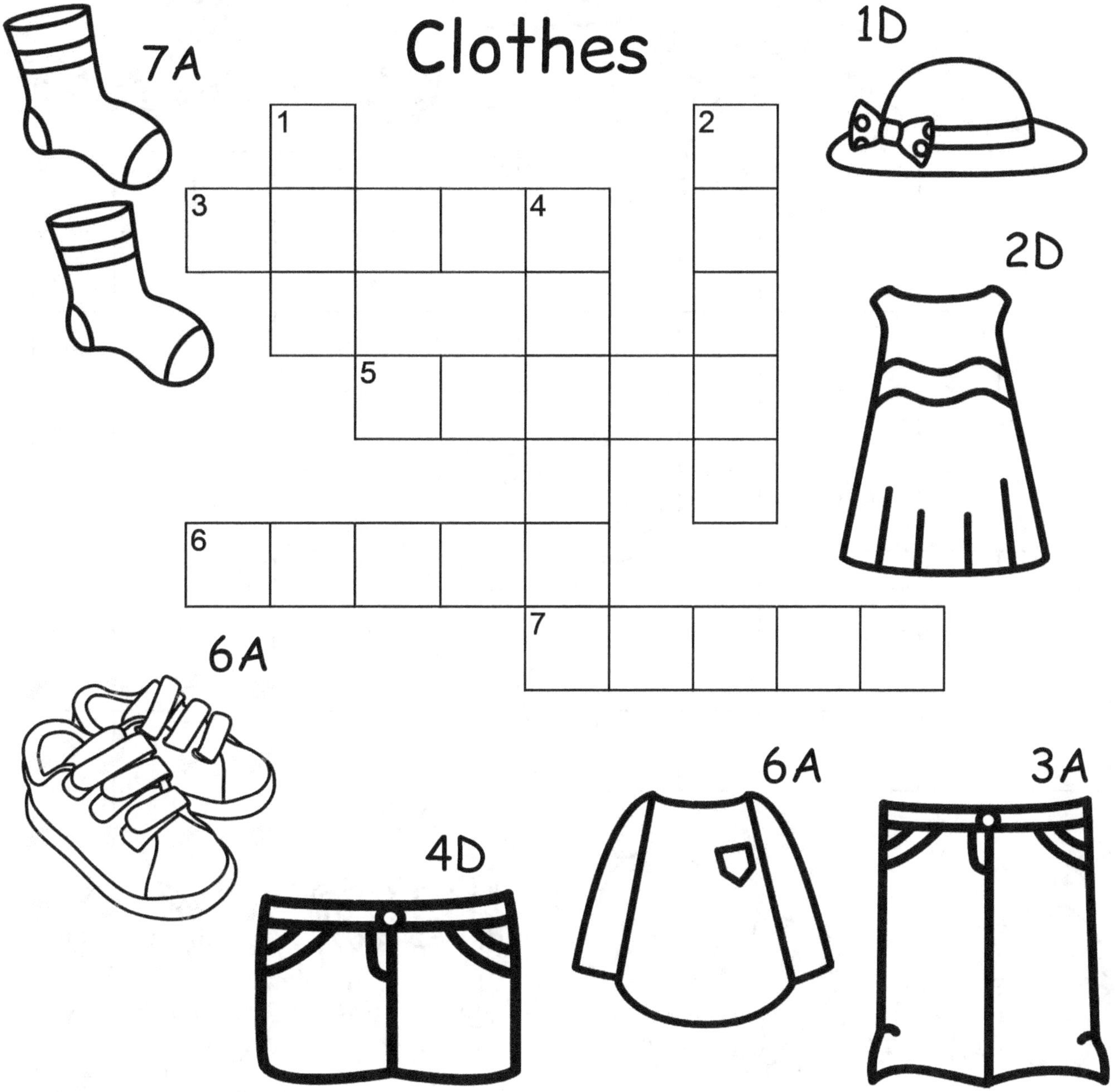

Animals At The Zoo

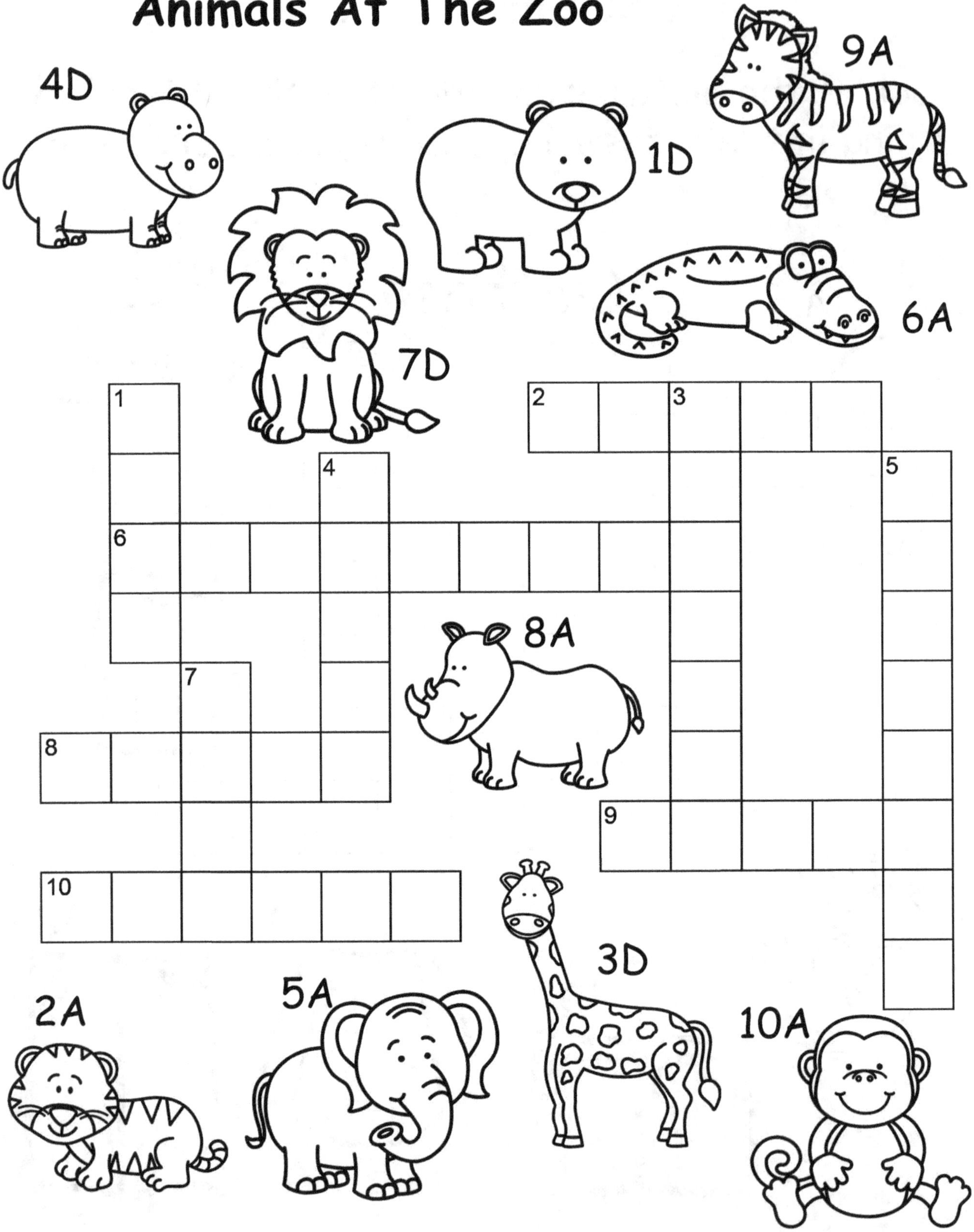

Animals In The Water

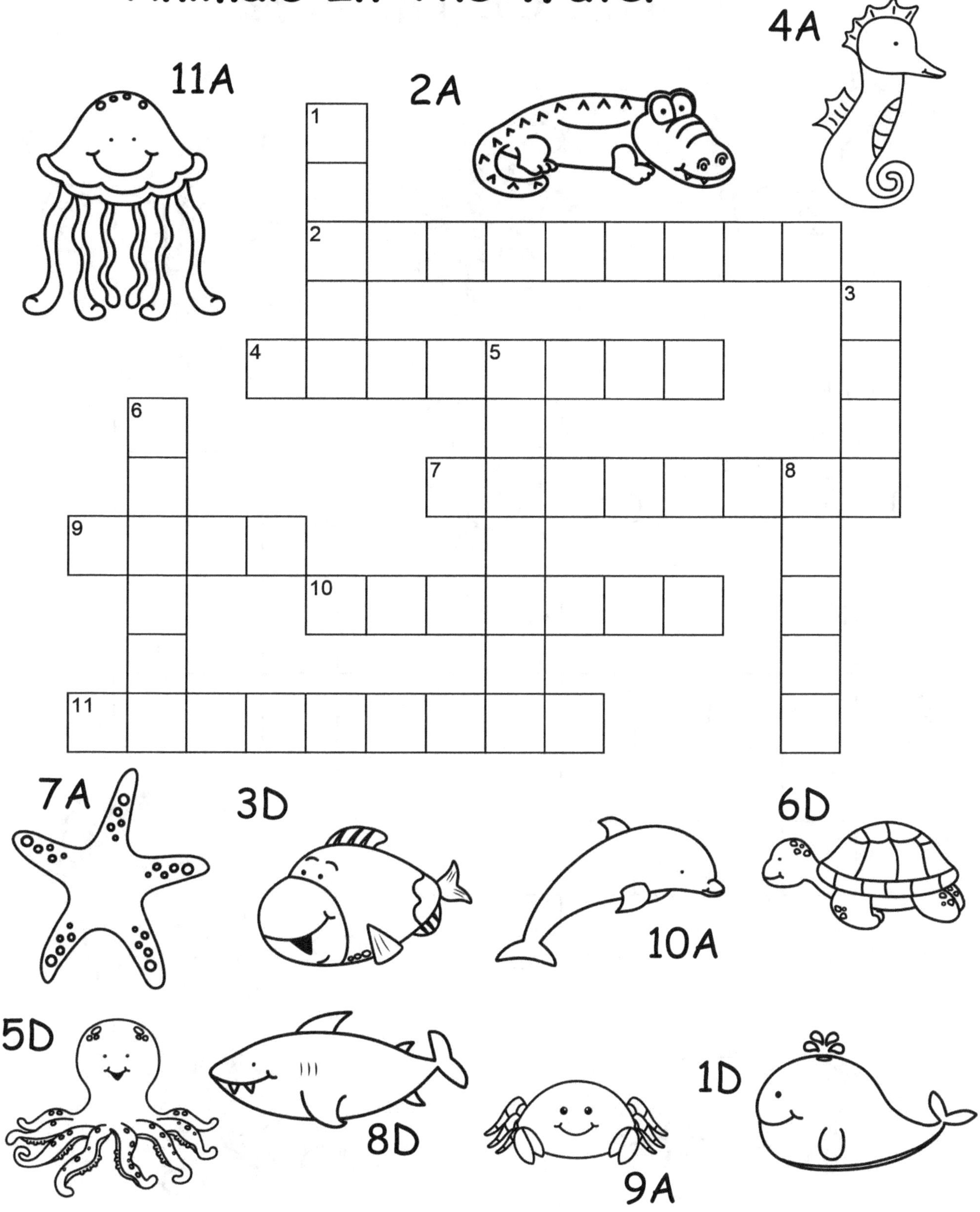

Animals On The Farm

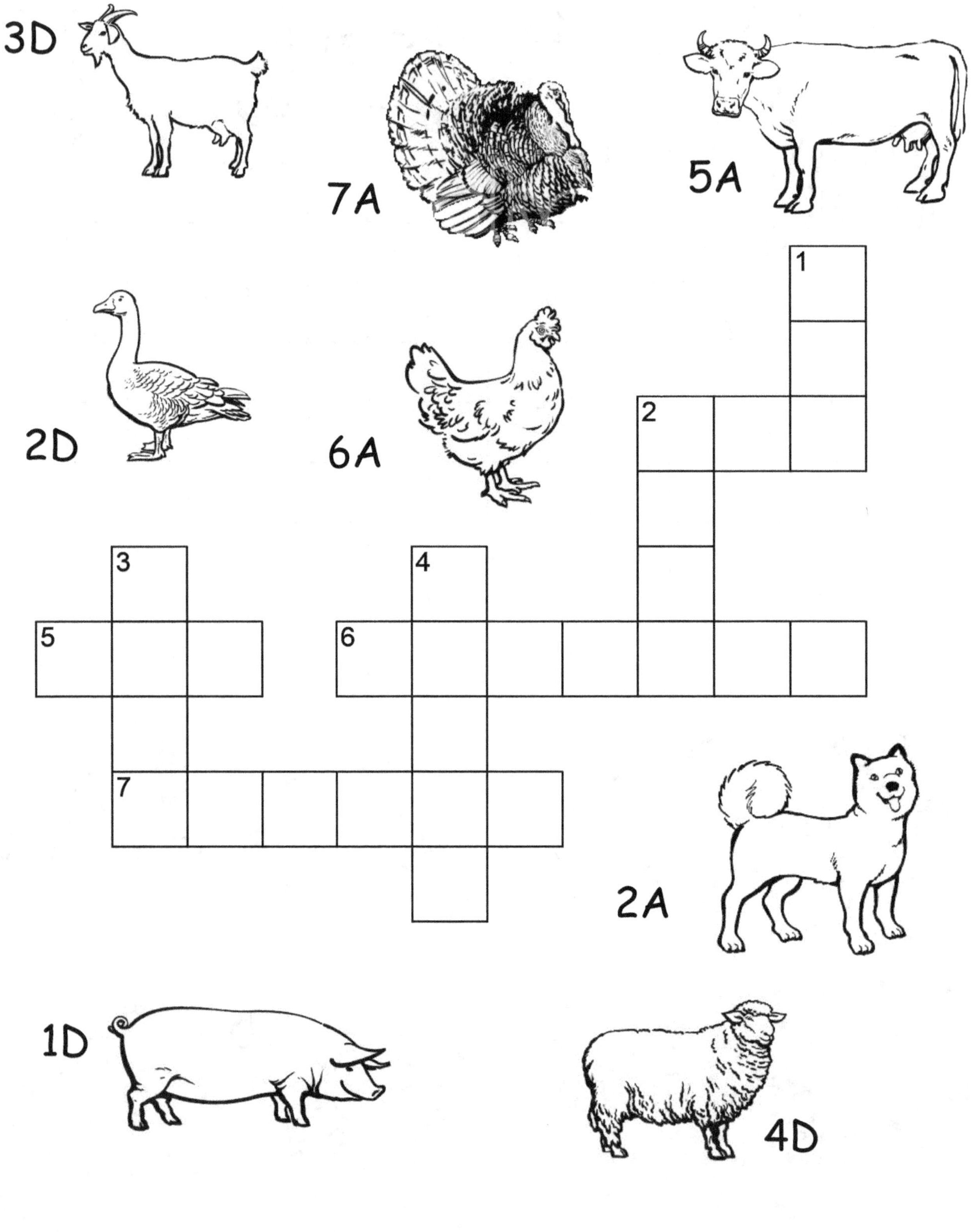

Bugs & Insects

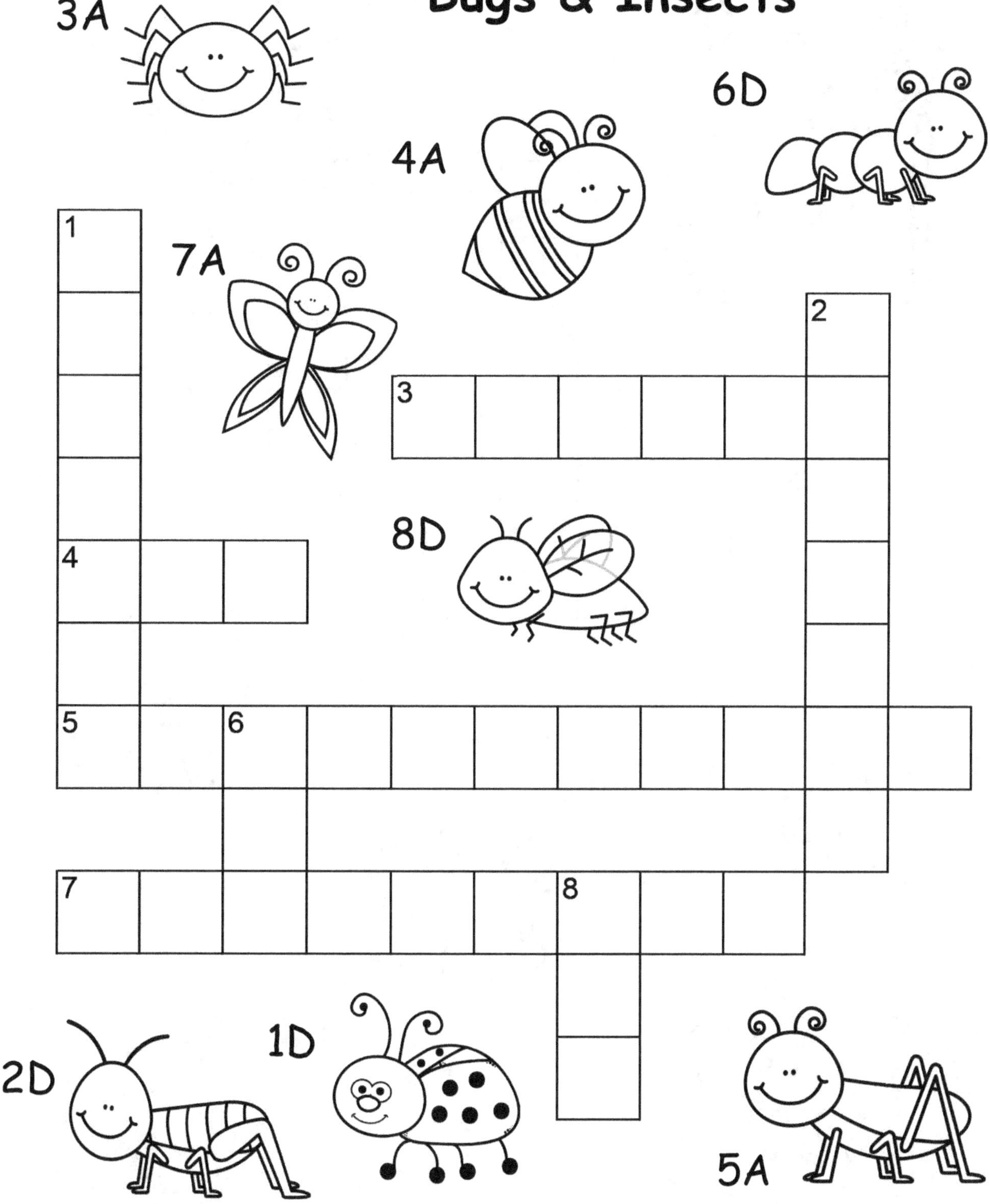

2D

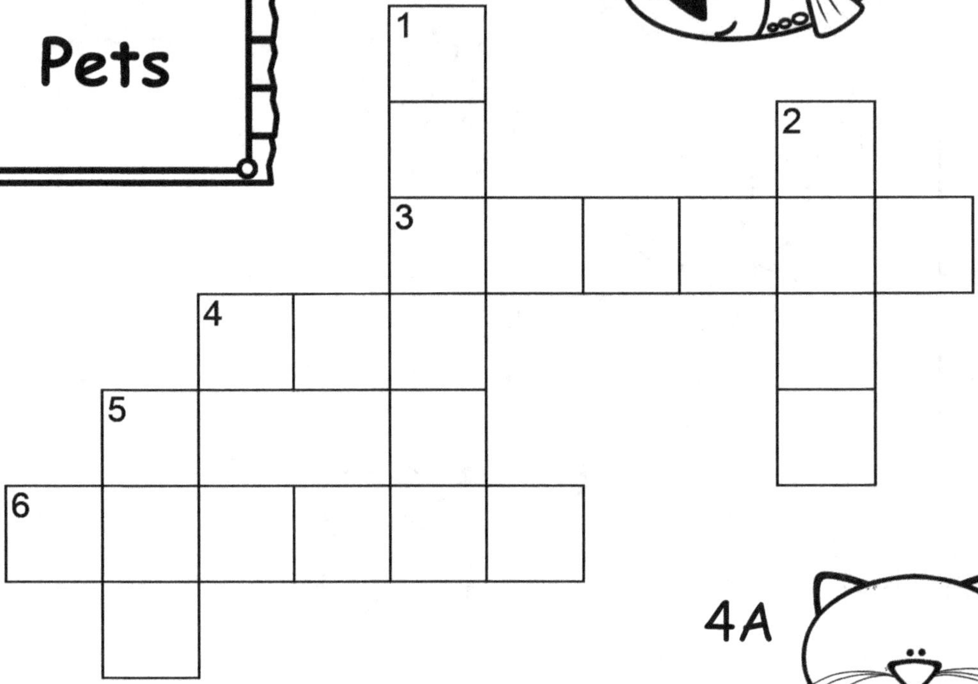

4A

1D

5D

6A

3A

Food

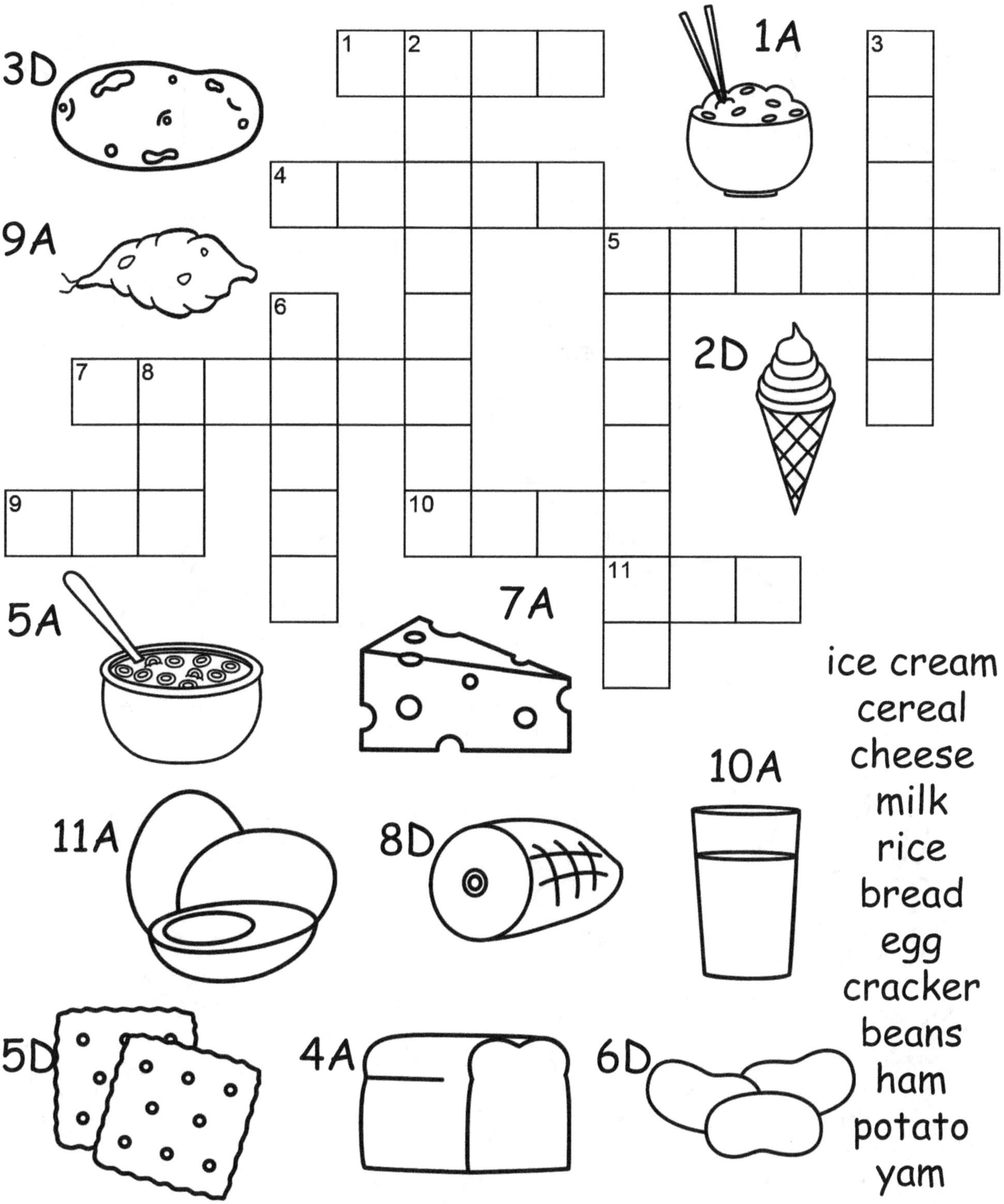

ice cream
cereal
cheese
milk
rice
bread
egg
cracker
beans
ham
potato
yam

Fruits and Veggies

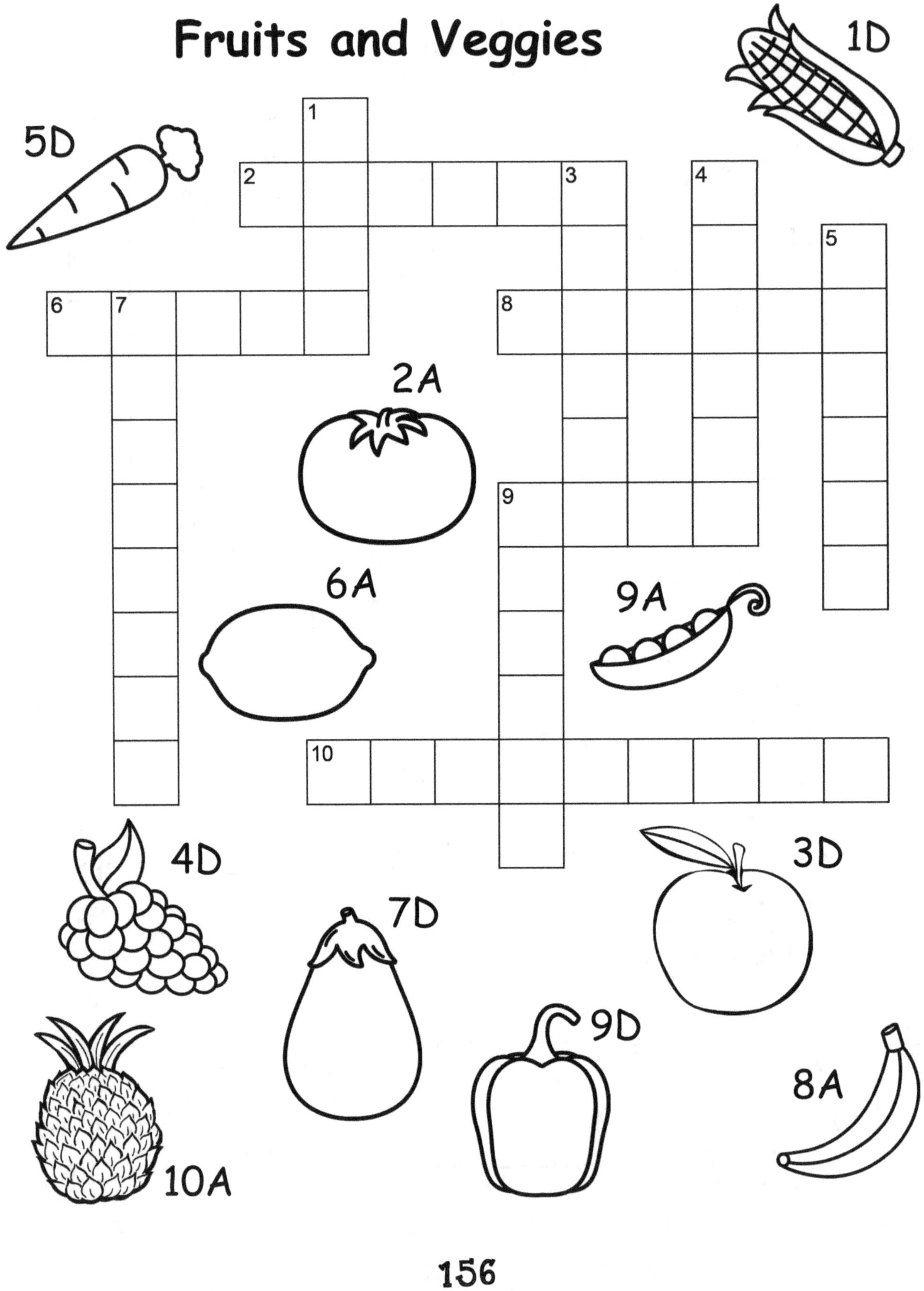

Transportation

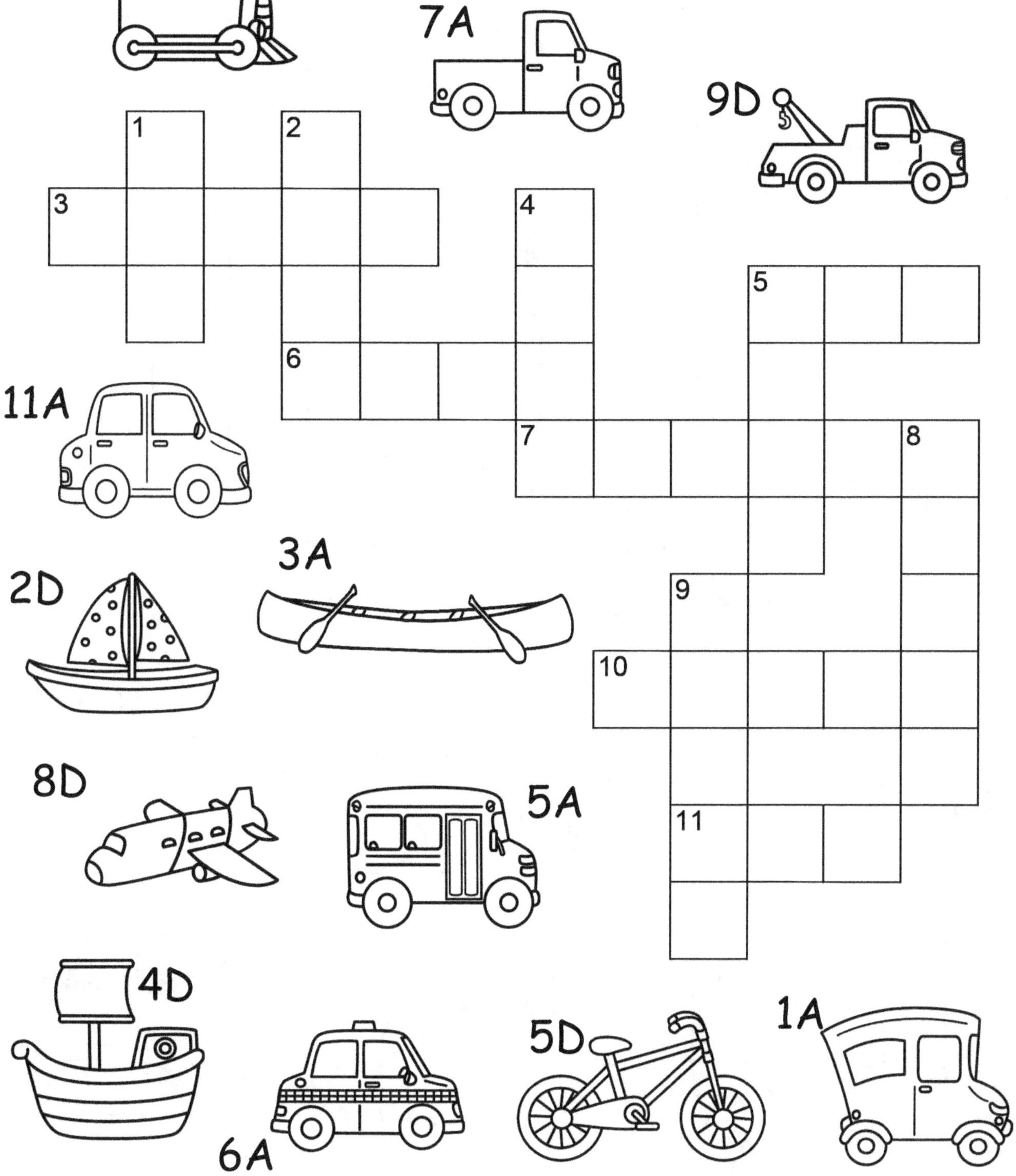

School Things

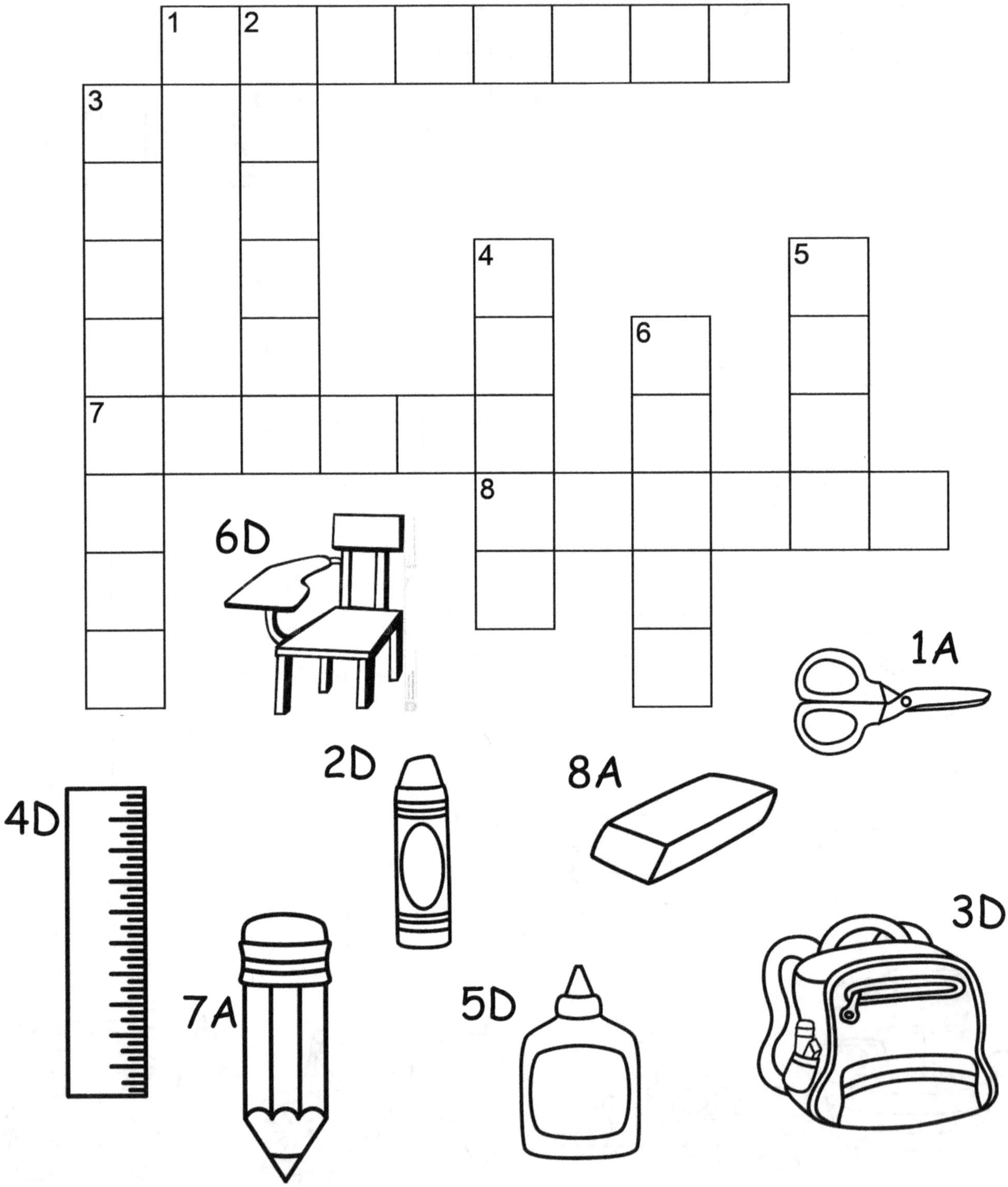

Going Shopping

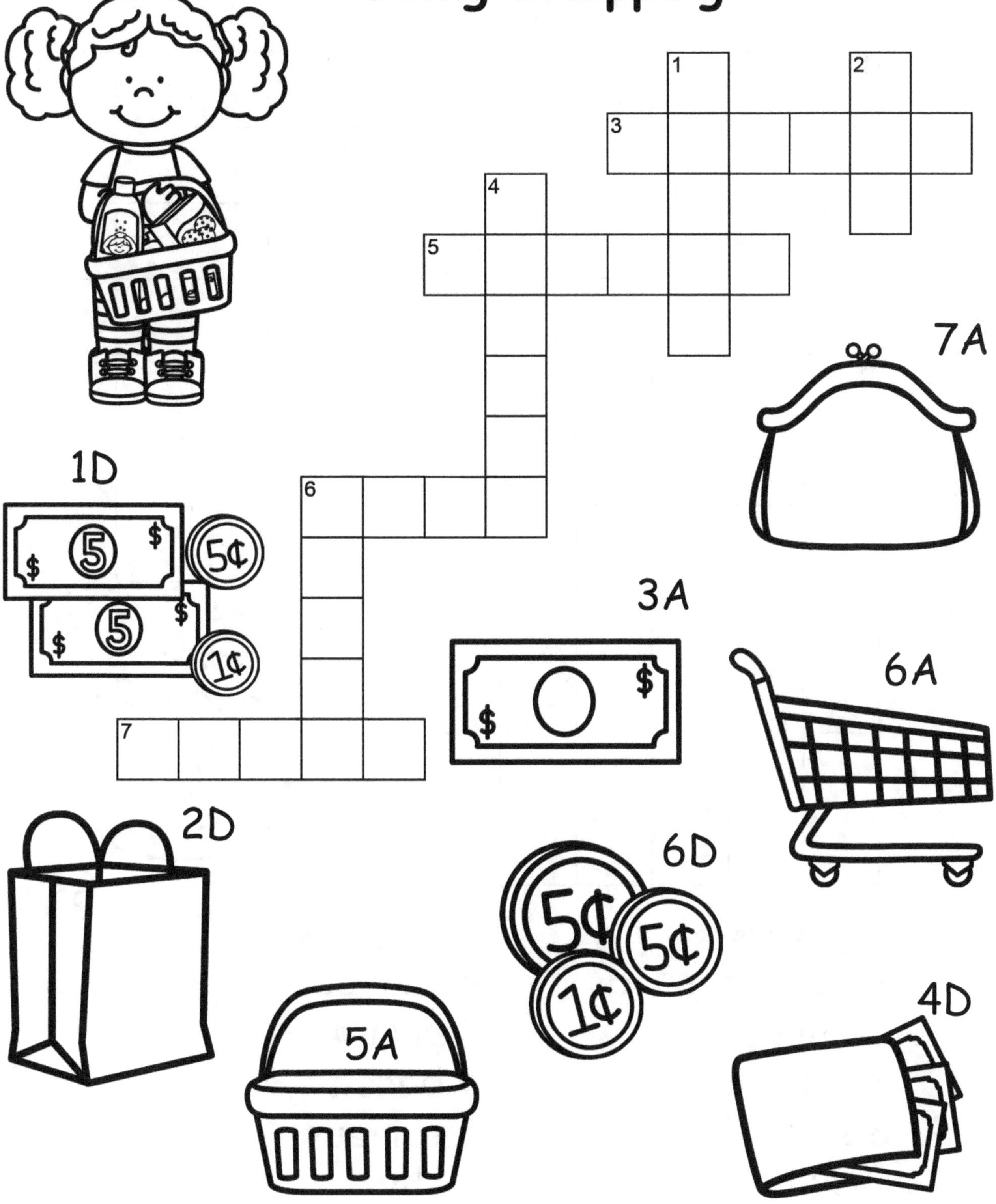

How Do You Feel Today?

9A

Across

1 embarrassed
3 happy
7 surprised
8 sad
9 silly

Down

2 scared
4 proud
5 bored
6 curious
8 shy

1A

6D

8D

5D

2D

4D

7A

8A

3A

9A

13A

7D

5D

8D

10A

4D

1D

2D

I Love My Family

Across

3 niece
6 husband
9 mother
10 grandma
12 aunt
13 father
14 uncle

Down

1 sister
2 nephew
4 brother
5 daughter
7 son
8 grandpa
11 wife

3A

12A

6A

14A

11D

Family Words

aunt
brother
daughter
father
mother
husband
son
niece
wife
uncle
sister
nephew

grandma
grandpa